NOW THAT'S WHY I GOT INTO TEACHING:
STUDENT VOICES FROM THE FRONT LINES OF PUBLIC EDUCATION

By
Robert Henry

Illustrations by Bouchra Houmaidi

Interior design and cover design by Rick Schank, Purple Couch Creative

Manufactured in the United States

Library of Congress Cataloguing-in-Publication Data has been applied for.

ISBN: 979-8-9881405-0-4 (hardback)

ISBN: 979-8-9881405-1-1 (paperback)

ISBN: 979-8-9881405-2-8 (ebook)

IF YOU HAVE BEEN IN AN URBAN PUBLIC SCHOOL in any capacity, these are stories and voices that will be all too familiar. Henry's stories of urban public schools are hilarious, insightful, and emotional. In an age of standardized testing, expanding technology, and politics of education, these stories remind us of the fundamental goals of education.

Don Luong
8th Grade History Teacher

Mom hates it when I act stupid.   I know, right? They're so annoying.

FOREWORD

PUBLIC EDUCATION SEEMS TO BE IN BAD SHAPE. COVID-19 exposed long-standing ills ranging from entrenched inequality for students to teachers' job dissatisfaction, which has only increased lately because of rising vitriol and politicization surrounding teachers and public education. Public education is always in critical condition, but the patient seems to be in worse shape than usual.

So it's time to step back and remind ourselves of some basic truths. To begin with, *teaching is a noble profession, one where adults continually and as a matter of routine touch children's hearts, minds, and souls.* This may seem obvious, but it is startling that something this profound isn't really publicly acknowledged very often. Second, most people get into and stay in teaching because something compels them to do so, not because teaching as a profession makes complete sense. As one marcher's sign declared during the 2019 strike by United Teachers of Los Angeles: "I'M IN IT FOR THE MONEY, said no teacher ever." Something else we seem to ignore is that good teachers love being around children and love the relationships they form with children. This book celebrates these facts and reminds us what they look and sound like.

The book is a collection of conversations between me and students and between the students themselves. I taught sixth grade in the Los Angeles Unified School District (LAUSD), and the genesis of the idea of writing down what students said was a fairly horrible event. I sat in my classroom during a conference period, which is a "free" period where teachers plan and correct papers and never have enough time to collaborate. In walked my team teacher, the teacher who taught math and science to the students I taught English and history.

"I was just in the Dean's office. Joyce got suspended," the teacher said.

"Makes sense."

"Her mother came to pick her up. Mom went up to her and said, 'Let's go, bitch.' Joyce said to her, 'Least I ain't the bitch that had the bitch.'"

That made me stop grading; even for the often harsh and bleak world that was LAUSD's Horace Mann Middle School at the time, this was noteworthy.

"You want to shock America, just write down what happens at this school," I said.

Said my team teacher, "You want to shock America, put web cams in the hallways of C block." 'C block' was the name we used for the "C" building (we were in "A" building), where the seventh and eighth graders had their classes, and it tells you what teachers thought of it.

Some of what's in this book is a reconstruction of things that stuck in my head, but much of it is conversations I scribbled down when I had the chance. The students spoke with a mixture of slang, newly learned English, Spanglish, and what many linguists call African-American English and Chicano English, languages that have their own rule-governed grammars. For those who love the ever-changing diction of English and its neighbor languages, listening to precisely how students say what they say is always entertaining. And because many of my students cursed as a matter of routine, there are f-bombs aplenty; to soften it or to write f---- would be to lie.

I was privy to and part of these conversations because for years I kept my room open to students at nutrition (recess) and lunch, and sometimes before school, and present and former students came into my room to get away from the madding crowd. I had few rules during this time other than, "Don't be an idiot and don't irritate me." I would chat with students, catch up on e-mails, and get ready for the next class—all the while listening to what the students were saying as they drew on the white board, played Foosball (a departing teacher gave me a full-sized Foosball table), graded papers for me, did their homework, played on their Chromebooks, or just hung out. Some days there might be a dozen students, some days two or three.

Other times I chatted with students as we lined up outside my classroom. At my second school, where I spent most of my years, I was always fortunate not to have a classroom in a hallway, so there was no rush to clear the hall and get students into class. As the children settled outside the classroom and took their time getting in line, I'd chat with them, catch up on their lives, listen to their complaints or observations, or answer their questions. At my second school there was also a lot of informal conversation during the dispersal of Chromebooks (web-only laptops) at the start of the day—first homeroom—and the collection of Chromebooks at the end of the day—second homeroom. Some of the conversations I overheard while walking down the halls or while outside on the yard.

These conversations will help readers see the world through the eyes of today's urban, economically-disadvantaged children of color, the population I taught. The conversations will remind everyone that education is not really about dispersing information: It's about relationships between students and teachers.

A Note On Names

To protect students' privacy, I have changed their names. When it doesn't make things more confusing, I use "S1" or "S2" to indicate a student or "FS" for a female student or "MS" for a male student when it seemed to me that gender influenced the conversation.

CONTENTS

Hey mister! My baby brother's only two, and he can already put up the middle finger and say, "Foo you!"

OVERVIEW

THE EMOTIONS TEACHERS FEEL AND FACE EVERY day range from humor to horror. Students say things which compel teachers to call the police and which make teachers laugh out loud. Two moments from my career sum this up.

It's the morning before the first day of school, and, as I'm writing vocabulary words for the first unit on 5"x7" index cards, a female student I had for sixth grade the previous year walks into my room.

FS: Hi, Mister. Anything I can do for you?

Me: Hey *[student's name]*, great to see you! Uh, well, sure, you can copy this list onto these cards. *[smiling]* Print neatly, okay?

FS: *[flatly]* Sure, Mister.

[I give her the materials, and she starts to do that.]

Me: I'm glad you stopped by! How was your summer?

FS: Oh, I don't know...

[As she works for a moment in silence, I sense that something is not right. I go over to where she's seated and crouch down across the table from her.]

Me: [student's name], what's going on? [She starts to cry. I take her hands.]

FS: [after a moment] Well...last week my stepfather tried to take my clothes off, so I grabbed a knife and threatened to stab him and stab myself.

Me: Oh. I'm so sorry that happened to you. You know what, stay right here and finish that for me, but then don't go anywhere, okay? I go directly to the main office, find the administrator who is the dedicated reporter for suspected child abuse, and tell her; as she heads to my room I call the Los Angeles Police Department and start filling out the required forms.

Or, the time I'm ushering students into the classroom at the start of the day as the last bell rings.

A female student has been outside the door talking to friends from a different class, and upon hearing the bell, she sprints to the room but stops abruptly when she sees me.

FS: Mister! You got a haircut! Finally!

That's teaching: the horrifying and the endearing.

For what follows, it will help if the reader knows a little about me and my classroom. I don't know if I was an especially effective teacher, and I don't know what my style was exactly, but "Mr. Henry's Ten Commandments," posted at the front of my room, summed up my philosophy.

Mr. Henry's Commandments

I.   Read, Stop, Think, Respond

II.   Make Yourself Look Good And Sound Smart

III.   Read It Over Before You Turn It In

IV.   Once It's Good, Make It Interesting

V.   Remember That You Came Here Today To Make Mistakes

VI.   People With Power And Money Rarely Help People With Bad Manners

VII.   Don't Stop Somebody Else From Being Great

VIII.   Read Something Every Day

IX.   Effort X Ability = Skill

X.   Skill X Effort = Achievement

That was my philosophy, which evolved over time, of course. And who were the students? Well, at the start of every year, as an introduction to the concept of chronology for History class, I had students do a personal timeline, which would later be the basis for a personal memoir about one event. I had them write the three best things and three worst that happened to them and place them on a timeline. The worst things ranged from "watching my father shoot my mother" to "broke my skateboard," and the best things ranged from "got a puppy" to "my brother got out of prison." In other words, teachers in inner-city middle schools typically teach children who have had wonderfully commonplace upbringings and children who have had devastatingly horrible things happen to them.

That being said, here's a broad sampling of what children say and do away from their parents.

- You eat spicy chips now?
- You barely noticed? I've been eating them forever.

Justine: Mr. Henry, Louise got kissed at lunch! It was only on the cheek, though.

Louise: But I still have to take a shower!

I call on Bruce to answer a question, but Diego blurts out the answer.

Monica: *[to Diego] Callate!* You weren't called on!

Diego: I provided assistance. It's called *helping*.

FS1 comes up to my desk as FS2 sits in the classroom correcting papers for me during lunch.

FS1: Mister, somebody has a crush on me. What should I do?

Me: *[having no clue]* Well...uh...I...uh...

FS2: *[piping up]* Decide if you want to encourage him or ignore him.

Me: *[relieved]* There you go.

FS1: Thanks, Mister.

Me: Any time.

Out of nowhere, as the class is working silently on a writing assignment, Juan gets up and walks over to me.

Juan: Mister, can I change seats? Diana is irritating me.

Me: No.

Juan: But she's really irritating me.

Me: Get used to it. Some girl will be irritating you the rest of your life.

Juan: Really?

Me: Could very well happen.

Juan: *[really thinking about it]* Wow. *[After a moment of reflection he gets back to work.]*

MS: Mister, are you older than Spongebob?

Me: Well, I've been around longer than he has, so, yes.

MS: You mean when you were a kid, there was no Spongebob?

Me: Nope.

MS: Oh, man, you ARE old. No offense, Mister.

Me: None taken.

MS2: Mr. Henry, how old are you?

Me: I'm sixty.

MS2: Wow. When you die, I'm going to your funeral.

MS1: Me, too!

MS3: Me, too!

And soon the whole class agrees that they're going to my funeral.

FS: Guess what I heard last night, Mr. Henry?

Me: I don't know.

FS: Gunshots. At three a.m. It woke me up!

Me: Was anybody hurt?

FS: I don't know. I went back to sleep.

We have read the Shel Silverstein poem "A Boy Named Sue," where a man tracks down the father who abandoned him, determined to kill him for naming him Sue.

Me: Okay, let's think of some of Sue's character traits. What words would we use to describe Sue? And read or paraphrase the words from the poem that show you're right.

S1: He's determined. It says he traveled from town to town to find his father. He didn't stop.

S2: He's tough. It says he got part of his ear cut off, and he didn't stop fighting.

S3: Sue weak. He shoulda shot his daddy when he had the chance.

After a student misbehaves in a profoundly age-inappropriate manner I reprimand him and give the class yet another inspirational talk about the benefits of not behaving in an anti-social manner. I conclude with:

Me: ...and because that leads to something that will land you in jail.

MS: *[to a classmate]* I've been to jail. It's pretty good. You make lots of friends.

A former student has spent a semester at another middle school, John Burroughs, which has students of a higher economic class. I see her back on campus for the first time.

Me: Hey, Sandy, good to see you. How was Burroughs?

Sandy: Those kids all so weak.

Me: Weak?

Sandy: They be doin' their classwork, their homework, gettin' to class on time...That's not me, Mr. Henry.

Me: Maybe it should be.

Sandy: Aw come on, Mr. Henry.

Me: How are your classes this year?

Sandy: Bad. I have all the dumb teachers.

Jovana, who is my Teaching Assistant, grades all my papers, and even has my password to take roll and clean up my online gradebook, comes into my eighth grade homeroom with Doug.

Jovana: Doug! Shut the fuck up!

Me: Jovana, watch your mouth.

Jovana: Sorry, Mr. Henry. But tell Doug to shut up. He's annoying.

Me: *[Doug really is annoying.]* Doug, shut up. You're annoying.

Me: *[speaking to the whole class]* So, the next writing assignment is what we call a personal memoir. It's going to be about one event in your life. One thing that happened to you. Think about the best or the worst thing that ever happened. The best or the worst. The more powerful it is in your mind, the easier it will be to write about.

Laura: That's easy. The worst thing I ever did was go back to live with my parents.

- Mister, do you play Fortnite?　　-No, I do not play Fortnite

Remember, he told us he only does real stuff.

James is a bratty boy and both students and teachers find him annoying. He's fairly aggressive, he thinks he's tough, and he's quick to pick on other students. Carla is an athletic girl whose father, after whom she was named, died the summer before the start of sixth grade. Carla and her father were very close, and she is dealing with the loss with an astounding degree of dignity—and with an underlying sadness that breaks your heart. She is always well-mannered and respectful, and it would be easy to believe that someone told her that the best way to honor her father would be to behave in a way that would make him proud.

One day towards the end of a period, Carla stands up, looks down at James in the seat next to her, and quickly and easily flips over his desk. He's lying on the floor, and she kneels down and starts punching him in the face. Students immediately circle around and watch.
Me: Carla, stop. *She doesn't. I'm in no hurry to stop her, and the students are happy to see James get hit.* Carla, stop. *She doesn't, but it's clear she's getting tired, and James has covered up and really isn't getting hurt, although he does start to cry. I walk over to her and gently place my hand on her shoulder.* Carla, stop. *She does.* Go stand

by my desk, please.

As she does so I look down at James and see that he's not badly hurt. You okay, James? *He continues crying. Then the bell for lunch rings.* Okay, everyone but Carla and James can leave. Don't forget to do your homework. *The class slowly starts to file out, and as I urge them to leave I turn to one of the students.* Gerald, please ask Mr. Smith to come here.

Gerald nods. Mr. Smith has the same students for different subjects, and his room is directly across the hall. James sits in a chair, trying to stop his tears as I go up to Carla.

Me: What's going on?

Carla: *[still seething]* He was talkin' 'bout my daddy. *[I believe her completely.]* You okay now? *[She nods.]* I'll talk to you later, all right? Go to lunch. Don't worry about this.

Mr. Smith walks in. I whisper to him what happened. We sit next to James.

Me: *[to James]* Are you hurt?

James: *[sniffling and wiping away the last of the tears]* No.

Me: Do you want to go to the nurse?

James: No.

Me: So you were talking about her father? *[He doesn't respond, so I assume it's true.]* If you want, we can go to the Dean right now, and we can report this. It's clear that she hit you first, so she'll probably get suspended.

Mr. Smith: And pretty soon the whole school will know you got beat up by a girl.

Me: Yep. In fact, that she really kicked your butt. But if you want to, we can go to the Dean right now.

James: No.

Mr. Smith: You're sure?

James: Yeah.

Me: Okay. You can go. *[James starts to walk out.]*

Mr. Smith: James. *[James stops.]* Unless you watch it, your mouth is gonna keep gettin' you beat up.

James walks out of the room. Mr. Smith looks at me.

Mr. Smith: Let me guess: one of those fights you take your time breaking up.

Me: Yep. He's such an asshole—and the whole school will find out, anyway. Who knows, maybe he'll learn.

Mr. Smith: Let's hope. You see the Lakers last night? Koh-bee!

I wasn't cussing, Mr. Henry, I was just voicing my thoughts.

THE SWEET CLASS

I HAD ONE GROUP OF STUDENTS AT JOHNNIE L. Cochran, Jr. Middle School that was the most wonderful group of eleven year olds anyone could hope to be around—a bunch of students I got to teach, not ones I got paid to teach. There were no budding sociopaths, no one who would, say, go on to get arrested for attempted murder, or be killed while robbing a liquor store after sixth grade, or father three kids before tenth grade—all of which happened to students of mine. This group liked and enjoyed each other. They misbehaved only in age-appropriate ways, and when they got a little rowdy, I'd just hold my hand up and say, "If you want nasty Mr. Henry to come out of his cave, I'll go get him," and they would calm down immediately.

They were all Latino English Learners, which meant they didn't speak English at home (but spoke Spanish) and had not proven proficiency in English, and they all qualified for the free lunch program. Almost all were immigrants, and several were Special Education students. While their academic skills weren't the highest, most of them sincerely tried to learn. Even at the end of the year, I continued to be amazed by their kindness, generosity, and grace. I could never figure out if this was what teaching sixth grade was supposed to be like, or if what I customarily experienced, where there were enough damaged children in the room to keep a dozen therapists busy, was the norm even outside of LAUSD.

Between the bells and time that end one period and start the next, one day the students are playing tag outside. The bell rings, and I call out to the students.
Me: Line up. No playing tag after the bell rings. *[They quickly line up.]*
Pablo: You're cool, Mr. Henry. Mrs. Smith won't let us play tag at all.
Me: I'm not cool. It's just that Mrs. Smith has never been an eleven-year-old boy, so she doesn't know how important it is sometimes to play tag. *[Pablo holds out his fist, and we bump fists.]*
Pablo: You're the best, Mr. Henry.
Me: No, I'm not. Mrs. Smith is a much better teacher, trust me.
Pablo: No way!
Me: Yes way. Now shut up and go inside.

During the time when the movie Batman v. Superman: Dawn of Justice *is about to come out, I have this conversation.*
Pablo: Who do you go for Mister, Batman or Superman?

Me: The whole thing is stupid. How can two good guys fight each other?

Pablo: I don't know, but they are. Who do you go for?

Me: The whole thing is stupid.

Pablo: Who do you go for?!

Me: Well, the only way Batman can win is to use kryptonite, right?

Pablo: I guess...

Me: So, I'm guessing Batman invents a Batgun that shoots kryptonite, and he kills Superman.

Pablo: So you're going for Batman.

Me: No, I'm just guessing what's going to happen.

Pablo: *[now totally exasperated]* Who. Do. You. Go. For?!!!

Me: Well, I always thought the whole Batman-inspired-by-a-bat-is-secretly-Bruce-Wayne thing was kind of stupid...

Pablo: *[to the whole class]* Mr. Henry is going for Superman!!!
Much discussion breaks out.

One morning bouncy, upbeat, delightful Mary comes in, even more upbeat than usual, holding a large paper cup from 7-11.

Mary: *[holding up the cup]* I got some coffee, Mr. Henry!

Me: *[thinking, that's the last thing this girl needs]* Great, Mary. That's exactly what you need.

Mary: I know! I love coffee! Can I get the breakfast?

Me: Sure.

Mary: Great! Annie, hold my coffee! *[She gives the cup to Annie and skips out.]* Ha-ha! Julie doesn't get to get the breakfast this morning!

[Mary skips out to go to the cafeteria to get the rolling carts that contain each classroom's breakfast, since LAUSD, in its infinite wisdom, had decided that serving the students breakfast in classrooms makes way

more sense than serving students breakfast in the, oh, I don't know, the cafeteria.

Soon she returns with the cart way too quickly, panting, having apparently run the whole way. She gets her coffee back from Annie.]

Mary: Thanks, Annie! I'll set up the breakfast, Mr. Henry! *[She starts unpacking the insulated bags and setting up the breakfast on the designated tables.]* Oh boy, burritos! I love burritos! *[And she sings to herself as she works.]*

We're reading a novel where the main character encounters three juvenile drug users.

Me: Look at the last sentence on page 116. Mary, please read it out loud. *[Mary reads it aloud.]* Thank you. Annie, what does the writer expect us to infer from that sentence?

Annie: That the guys are on drugs.

Me: Exactly. The writer doesn't come out and say it; you're supposed to figure it out. To infer it.

Alan: *[joining in]* Later the cop tells Pancho that the boys were on drugs. In case we didn't figure it out. He says they're on meth.

MS: *[shouting out]* That's what my brother uses! He went to jail, but now he's going into rehab!

It's the end of class, and Pablo tries to get out of his seat, except he has his backpack on while it's wrapped around his chair, so when he stands up he takes the chair with him.

Me: Pablo, sit down and take off your backpack.

[Mary and Annie go to him and help him get untangled.]

Mary: Trust me, Mr. Henry, this was always happening in fifth grade, too.

Annie: Mister, how do languages work?

Me: It's complicated, isn't it?

Annie: Yes! There's too many words!

Annie: *[quite sad]* Oh Mr. Henry…

Me: What, Annie?

Annie: I hate my backpack.

Me: Why?

Annie: It's my brother's old one. It makes me look like a boy.

Me: It's a very nice backpack.

Annie: No. It's horrible.

Me: No, it's nice.

Annie: That's nice of you to say, Mr. Henry, but it's horrible.

- Okay, who's absent today?
- Annamaria and Evelyn. And they're my best friends.

One day Annie, having seen the previous years' girls come in at lunch, asks if she can stay.

Annie: Mister, can I stay in at lunch?

Me: Sure.

MS: Can I stay, too?

Me: As long as you don't irritate me.

MS: Oh. Never mind.

I'm at my desk eating lunch and Patricia and Connie come in and stand in front of my desk.

Patricia: Connie's depressed.

Me: Connie, why are you depressed?

Connie: Nobody likes me.

Me: I think Patricia likes you.

Patricia: No, *like. Like*-likes. A boy.

Me: Oh. She's lucky.

Connie: Lucky??? I don't want to be alone my whole life!

The wall phone rings. It's not an outside phone so it's a call from the office or another classroom. I have a student trained to answer it who would say, "Room 501, student speaking. Mr. Henry is incredibly busy. How may I help you?" But I am near the phone this time, so I answer it. The students can hear only my end of the conversation.

Me: *[the room number]* 501.

Office Staff Member: Good afternoon, Mr. Henry. Please send Patricia to the office. She's going home early.

Me: How about me? Can I go home early?

OSM: No, Mr. Henry, you can't.

Me: Why not?

OSM: Because you can't.

Me: But that's not fair. She gets to go home early.

OSM: No, Mr. Henry, it's not fair. I don't get to go home early, either. Bye, Mr. Henry. *[She hangs up, and I hang up. I turn to the class.]*

Me: Get your stuff, Patricia; you're going home.

Patricia: *[with a fist pump]* Yesssss!

Me: I never get to go home early.

Connie: If you did, you'd just play golf, and golf is stupid. So what's the big deal?

After P.E., the students are lining up. The sun has come out after a rainstorm.

Me: Ahhhh, a beautiful day after all.

Alex: Not for me.

Me: Why?

Alex: During P.E. I stepped in a hole.

Me: And you got wet.

Alex: And muddy! I had to take my sock off. *[He holds up a filthy sock.]*

Connie's Chromebook has broken, and we've learned it is going to take a few days to get it fixed. We're deciding what to do, when one student suggests that she use the Chromebook that had been used by a student who has just left the school.

Alex: Mister, can't she just use Jorge's Chromebook?

Me: We had to turn it in because he left the school.

Mary: He left the school because he got beat up by a girl! *[The class laughs.]*

Me: No, he moved.

Alex: Yeah, but he did get beat up.

Patricia: He wouldn't have gotten beat up if he knew how to fight. *[The class murmurs in agreement, discussing Jorge, and everyone agrees that he was a lover, not a fighter, and that's why he got beat up.]*

Caitlin: I cried when he left.

Mary: He cried when he left! *[Everyone laughs, and the class notices that I'm smiling and nodding my head with a strange look on my face.]*

Patricia: Mister, what is it?

[I'm thinking about Jorge's last day, when he came back to turn in his textbooks. He stopped by the room, and I asked him if he wanted to say good-bye to the class, and he said he did, and he got in front of the class to say good-bye, but then he got choked up and couldn't say anything. He turned and hugged me and cried.]

Me: Nothing.

Alex: Mister, you look sad!

Me: No, not sad. Here's a new word for you: reflective. *[I write it on the board, in syllables, and we all say it together.]* Re-flec-tive. Reflective. It's when you think about something. Jorge was a very nice boy, and we liked him, even loved him, and when you think about him, you're being reflective.

[The class is silent, nodding, thinking about Jorge.] Yeah, right now we're all being reflective.

Patricia has been absent a day, during which time, in our unit on Mesopotamia, students were given chunks of clay and rollers and small carving devices, and they had to write their names in cuneiform, the ancient script of Mesopotamia.

Connie: You're back! But you missed it! We wrote our names in clay in cuneiform! It was great!

Patricia: *[sadly]* Oh...

Connie: Mister, let's do it again, so Patricia can do it!

Me: No; we're going on to cover Hammurabi and his code of laws.

Alex: Mister, it's not fair to Patricia! *[much grumbling in the class]*

Me: *[after a moment, as the class is staring at me—they've learned that with them I'm actually a softie]* All right... Mary, Connie, please pass out the aprons and the rollers and the styluses; I'll get the clay. *The class cheers, and Patricia smiles.*

FS1: Why were you running after me?

FS2: I don't know. Why were you running away?

FS1: Because you were running after me!

FS2: Yeah, but you didn't have to run.

FS1: But *you* were!

FS2: So?

FS1: So? What? You're confusing me.

FS2: Never mind.

We're studying Ancient China in History class, preparing to watch part of a documentary about Emperor Qin Shihuangdi, and his image is on the screen. Pablo walks by the screen.

Pablo: Hey look! An Asian guy!

Bruce: He's Chinese, dumbass.

Pablo: China is in Asia, so he's Asian, double dumbass!

[Later in the movie, the Emperor prepares to draw-and-quarter his mother's lover, who has plotted to overthrow him.]

Patricia: Mister! Is this real?!

Me: Well, this sort of thing really happened. Many civilizations used this method to execute people. Why would leaders execute people like this instead of using a way that isn't so horrible?

Patricia: To send a message! He's saying, 'Go against me, and this is what happens.'

Me: That's it. But don't worry. They're not going to show it.

Most of the class starts shouting, "Show it! Show it! Show it!"

Then, as the traitor screams, the camera focuses on just the ropes the horses are pulling, and the ropes go taut. The students only see the taut ropes, but there is silence in the room. The scene immediately ends, having shown only the ropes, and the class, a second ago totally bloodthirsty, sits in silence, stunned.

Also while we're studying Ancient China.

Me: So how old was Prince Zheng when he became king? *[The whole class shouts out, "13!"]* So most of you are twelve now. Imagine, next year, one of you is king or queen of California.

FS: I'd say, 'No homework!'

Me: Seriously. Think about that. You'd be as old as Prince Zheng, so one of you is running the state. Man, I'd be out of California so fast.

FS2: But I'm very mature. And responsible. I'd be a good queen.

Me: Sorry, but I'd be gone.

FS2: Mr. Henry!

Me: Imagine. Imagine... *[I look around the room and point to a student.]* Angel is king of California.

FS2: Yeah, I'm leaving.

MS: No, I'm staying! He'd let us play Fortnite all day.

Angel: *[thinking about it]* Yeah, I would. *The boys cheer for King Angel.*

Class has just started, and the students are working on their 'Do Now' or 'Sponge' or 'Dispatch' assignment, the first task of the day, intended to get the students quiet and settled. The lone failing student, Stanley, as usual is not doing anything. He tests at a relatively high reading level, but he rarely does any work. His parents and I have had many conversations, and they have admitted that they have no idea what to do.

By this time in the school year I've taught the students the concept of under/over betting and 'the line', which we have often used when trying to guess the outcome of some future event. 'Cochran Cash' is an incentive program the school uses to reward students.

Me: Stanley, come on, get to work. *[I turn to a girl near me and whisper to her.]* How many times will I say that this period? What's the line?

FS: *[after thinking about it]* Five.

Me: I'm taking the over. Got any Cochran Cash?

FS: Yeah.

Me: How about a bet?

FS: Sure. *[We shake on it. I quickly forget all about it, and the class continues. After the bell rings I excuse the students. The FS comes up to me with a piece of Cochran Cash.]*

FS: Here, Mr. Henry. It was nine.

Me: *[surprised]* No, keep it. I was kidding.

FS: *[putting the paper on my desk]* Nope. A bet's a bet.

MS1: You gonna help your brother?

MS2: No, I don't like him right now. His friend can beat him up.

MS1: Your brother *is* kind of a jerk.

MS2: No, he's a real jerk.

Some students come into the room after P.E.

Me: How was P.E.?

Rachel: Oh Mr. Henry! We played mosquito!

Me: What's mosquito?

Rachel: It's like tag, but five kids in the class had plastic tubes, and those were their stingers.

Me: I get it.

Rachel: They chased after us and tried to sting us. It was so scary! And then when I was running away, I tripped and fell on my tushy-tushy!

Mr. Henry, is your favorite word 'knucklehead'?

Students are milling around during lunch. Mary corners a huge cockroach.

Mary: Mr. Henry, can I kill it?

Me: If you want. *[She steps on it.]* Now its friends are going to track you down.

Mary: *[as she puts it in the trash]* I'm not afraid of cockroaches.

Me: What if there's a million of 'em after you?

Mary: Mr. Henry! Why would you say that?! *[Rachel comes in; Mary turns to her.]* I killed a cockroach! Want to see it?!

Second homeroom. Students are on their Chromebooks, enjoying a few minutes of free time before they have to turn in the computers.

Rachel: I heard Justin Bieber is going out with Selena Gomez again. That's not right. She's older.

Timothy: Why does everybody hate Justin Bieber, anyway? They must be jealous.

Rachel: Who's older: Selena Gomez or Justin Bieber?

Timothy: I'll look it up. *[He does so.]* She's 25 and he's 23.

Rachel: That's wrong! She's older!

Diego: I really liked that one song of his...

Rachel: Mr. Henry, you got a new shirt!

Me: No, I just haven't worn this one in a while.

Rachel: Are you sure it isn't new?

Me: I'm sure.

Rachel: 'Cuz usually if you don't wear a Cochran shirt you wear that blue one or that checked one.

Me: Right. So make an inference and tell me why I'm not wearing either of those.

Rachel: *[she thinks, then triumphantly]* Because they're dirty!

And we bump fists.

Justine: Mr. Henry, how do you decide which watch to wear?

Me: What do you mean?

Justine: Well, you wore that one a lot, and then you weren't wearing it for a while, and now you're wearing it again. How do you decide?

Me: I don't know. Whichever one strikes my fancy.

Justine: What?

Me: Strikes my fancy. English language idiom. Means it feels good at that moment.

Justine: Strikes my fancy...I like that.

Mary: You've never worn that shirt before, Mr. Henry.

Me: My wife gave it to me for my birthday.

Justine: It looks good on you. You should keep wearing it.

For Christmas I got a belt with a guitar-shaped buckle, and I wore it to school.

Rachel: *[to Justine]* Look at Mr. Henry's belt!

Justine: That's cool. Hey everybody, look at Mr. Henry's new belt! *There's much examination and approval.*

Mary: Mister, you got new shoes!

Me: No, I just haven't worn these in a while.

Rachel: That's right. He wore those at the start of the year.

Mary: Mister, you didn't wear a tie!

Me: It's college awareness day. That's why the sweatshirt.

Mary: Oh. *[thinking]* You can't wear a tie in college?

Rachel: You like that tie, don't you, Mr. Henry?

Me: Why do you say that?

Rachel: You wear it a lot.

Me: You're right. What did you just do? *[She's puzzled.]* In terms of figuring something out.

Rachel: *[thinking, then proudly]* I made an inference!

Patricia: Mister, how do you decide which jacket to wear?

Me: What do you mean?

Patricia: Well, you either wear the brown one or the white one, but how do you decide which one?

Me: If it's colder, I wear the brown one.

Patricia: Oh.

I show the class an excerpt from Admiral William H. McRaven's commencement address at the University of Texas, an inspirational video I have shown several times to every class. In the excerpt the Admiral starts off by saying, 'If you want to change the world, start by making your bed.' He finishes by saying that one person actually can make a difference and change the world. When the video stops:

Alex: Who wants to change the world?! It's perfect just the way it is!

The central activity of this class, and for several years of every class, was reading. At one point in my career, after initial reading assessments had consistently shown that my typical entering student (coming into sixth grade) read below a third grade level, I threw out everything I had been doing and everything I was supposed to do.

I said to myself, "Screw it. Let's just get these children reading at something close to grade level."

So, we read a lot every day, and some days that was all we did. We read in English class, and we read in History class. Students did the Drop Everything And Read activity at least once every day for twenty minutes and then answered an open-ended question about what they read (and they could read anything they wanted); we read along to a recording; we did group (choral) reading; we used what is called Cloze reading or Stop/Write reading. We used the online reading programs Read Theory and Achieve 3000. Homework was the same every night: read for twenty minutes. We didn't write much. We didn't have any tests other than reading assessments. We didn't do Socratic Circles or K-W-L charts or Vocabulary Lists or Reciprocal Teaching or Group Work or notebook checks or spelling tests or Cornell notes or any other strategies recommended by highly-paid consultants or expensive district-wide programs. We just read.

I kept detailed records of their reading assessments, and I was supported by our terrific librarian, who found books for every student's interest and who agreed with me that all reading is good reading. On average, over the years that I ignored all directives and we did almost no preparation for the state tests, classes typically increased reading scores over two-and-a-half grade levels, and the Sweet Class increased over three-and-a-half grade levels. Forty percent of my students left reading at grade level (7th grade), which was unheard of for this population, and I had one student who entered sixth grade reading at a first-grade level and left at a seventh-grade level.

These are typical comments by students:

- "Mister, can we read *The Last Summer of the Death Warriors* today?!"
- "Mister, can we read *The Circuit* today?!"
- "Mister, can we read *Breaking Through* today?!"
- "Mister, can we read *The Skin I'm In* today?!"
- "Mister, can we read *Monster* today?"
- "Can I take this book home and finish it?"
- "I love this book!"
- "Ohhh, do we have to stop reading now?"
- "Mister, I never liked reading before, but now I do!"
- "This book is so good!"

Hey, give me a Snickers so I can have an allergic reaction
and go to the nurse and get sent home.

THE LUNCH BUNCH

THE CONVERSATIONS IN THIS SECTION COME from a group I later dubbed 'The Lunch Bunch' because when I had them for sixth grade they often stayed in for lunch, and then in seventh grade they came to my room for lunch nearly every day.

These were the leaders of the group.

- Laura was being raised by her grandmother because of her parents' drug use.
- Hilda finished sixth grade reading at an eleventh-grade level. In both sixth and seventh grade she was my T.A., correcting papers and setting up the room.

- Nickie wasn't my student, but she was friends with the other girls, so she came to the room during lunch.
- Monica was an undocumented immigrant who had been held back a year in elementary school. Partly because she was a year older, she was taller, calmer, and more mature than the other students. On the day after the 2016 presidential election, she was waiting outside my door when I arrived and said to me, "Mister, am I going to get deported?"

Diego: Mr. Henry, you didn't write the schedule right on the board. You forgot lunch.

Me: I didn't forget. Lunch has been cancelled today. *[There's much uproar in the room.]* No, really. Students were acting too crazy at lunch, so it's been cancelled. Like I say, you get treated the way you act. *[The uproar gets even louder. I turn to Hilda and whisper quietly.]* Hilda, do you believe that?

Hilda: Of course not. Are teachers going to give up lunch?

I'm in the room eating lunch, and Laura walks in.

Laura: Mister, I'm bored. Can I clean the room?

Me: Knock yourself out.

Laura: Thanks. I do it at home all the time, so it's nothing.

[Laura grabs the broom and dustpan and starts sweeping the room. Monica walks in and sees what she's doing.]

Monica: You bored?

Laura: Yep.

Monica: Let me help.

The two girls clean the room.

Monica: Mr. Henry, what's your favorite song?

Me: Oh, I don't know. What's yours?

Monica: 'Oh, What A Beautiful Morning.'

Me: [*not believing her*] Really? How does it go?

Monica: Umm...The canyon is standing like statues, something about corn...

Me: Just sing the chorus. The part that repeats.

Monica: [*singing quickly, easily, correctly*] 'Oh what a beautiful morning, oh what a beautiful day, I've got a beautiful feeling, everything's going my way.'

Me: Perfect! The other part is cattle, not canyon. The *cattle* are standing like statues.

Monica: [*not sure*] Cattel?

Me: Cat-tle. Cows.

Monica: Oh, that makes sense! It didn't make sense before!

Monica walks up to me during lunch.

Monica: Mr. Henry! I hate sports!

Me: No, you just haven't found the right one yet.

Monica: My mother has made me try them all, believe me. First it was soccer. Then volleyball. Then basketball! Well, I kind of liked volleyball.

Me: So?

Monica: Well, I had to meet new people, and I hate that!

Monica: Mister, what are you eating?

Me: Macaroni and cheese.

Monica: But you left off the best part, the cheese.

Me: This has white cheese.

Monica: White cheese? Why would you do that?

Me: That's the way it came.

Monica: I like it with... *[Which word is right?]* Is it yellow cheese or orange cheese?

Me: Usually orange cheese.

Monica: Yeah, that's right. The oranger the better.

[Laura walks up]

Laura: Mister, what are you eating?

Monica: It's macaroni and cheese with white cheese!

Laura: *[stunned]* Wow...I've never seen that before. It doesn't look right.

Monica: I know! It looks like there's no cheese!

Laura: *[still trying to take it all in]* Wow...

Nickie: Mr. Henry, can you heat up my *pupusas*?

Me: Sure, I can, but what's it to you?

Nickie: Would you?

Me: Maybe if you ask properly.

Nickie: Mr. Henry, would you please heat up my *pupusas*?

Me: Happy to. *[I put them in my microwave.]* Did your mom make these?

Nickie: Yep. She made them especially for my brother. But he woke up late. So, they're mine.

Diego: Mr. Henry, I'm hungry, and you're eating in front of me.

Me: Well, go to the cafeteria and get something to eat.

Diego: But I don't like the food there! What is that, anyway?

Me: Pasta with salmon sauce.

Diego: Salmon? Like the fish?

Me: Yep.
Diego: [*trying to comprehend*] Wow…

Monica: Mr. Henry, you're eating in front of me again.
Me: It's lunchtime. What am I supposed to do?
Monica: But you always eat such good food! And they serve terrible food here!

Monica: [*out of nowhere*] Mr. Henry, did you see *The Girl on the Train?*
Me: No.
Monica: It was too sexual! No one told us, and we went inside, and it was horrible!

The students return to my class after P.E. and line up to go inside. Hilda is first in line.
Me: How was P.E.?
Hilda: It was horrible. We played softball.
Me: Softball's fun!
Hilda: Mr. Henry, softball's hella boring! Soccer's way better.
Me: Well, that may be true. But softball's more fun than math.
Hilda: Well, of course!

A couple girls have brought cupcakes and they're debating where to put them in the room so no one will get them. One girl suggests putting them on a high shelf that isn't very big.
Laura: They might fall. Then no one will eat them.

Monica: Yes they will. You know the boys.

During lunch several of the girls are in the room. Monica is sitting closest to my desk as I my lunch.

Me: Monica, you want some of this candy?

Monica: Sure! Where'd you get it? In the faculty lounge?

Me: God no. In an Easter basket. From my wife.

Monica: Oh, that's so sweet!

Me: She's a very sweet woman.

Monica: Oh, Mr. Henry...[*She looks very touched and starts to eat the candy.*]

Me: You know, you could share that with Laura. It won't kill you.

Monica: It will kill me! When it comes to my food, I never share!

- Remember this book?!   - Yeah. It had too many words.

Monica: Mr. Henry, do you pray?

Me: Sure.

Monica: I fall asleep when I pray. That's why I don't pray. I don't mind going to church for funerals or weddings, those I appreciate, but otherwise...

This took place in 2016.
Laura: Mister, do you like The Nirvanas?
Me: That's not the name of the band.
Laura: What?
Me: The band. It's not called, 'The Nirvanas.'
Laura: Oh. What's it called?
Me: Nirvana. Just Nirvana. *[I sing]* 'Here we are now entertain us. Acting stupid, entertain us.'
Laura: *[singing]* 'He's the one who likes all our pretty songs, and he likes to sing along, and he likes to shoot his gun / But he knows not what it means.'
Me: You're living in the past, Laura.
Laura: I love the past!

Hilda: My dad's mad at me because I want to listen to AC/DC, and my mom's mad at me because I always act like a boy.
Monica: No you don't.
Hilda: I always wear big, baggy clothes and I don't wear bright colors, and she says that's a boy.

Laura: Mister, why do girls get in *[with derision]* relationships?
Me: Because they're stupid.
Laura: I thought so!

We're walking back from the school library, and I'm chatting with Laura.

Laura: Mister, where are you from?

Me: I was born in San Francisco.

Laura: Lucky!

Me: Why? Where were you born?

Laura: Here.

Me: Los Angeles?

Laura: Yeah, not Mexico or anything.

Me: You don't like being born in Los Angeles?

Laura: No!

Me: What's wrong with Los Angeles?

Laura: The schools are all ghetto, and, I don't know...I just wish I was born in your country.

Me: San Francisco and Los Angeles are in the same country. The USA. Even the same state. California.

Laura: Oh. Well, I still wish I was born in San Francisco.

Monica: I'm sorry I couldn't stay during lunch, Mr. Henry, but those boys came in, and I've hated them since fifth grade.

Nickie and Monica are drawing on the board during lunch. Nickie turns to Monica.

Nickie: When you grow up, you're going to marry Diego and you're going to have one kid and it's going to be great.

Monica smiles.

Laura is passing out the Chromebooks, and as she walks by Pedro, she

slugs him on the shoulder. He reacts very calmly.
Pedro: *[to Laura]* Why'd you hit me?
Laura: That was for yesterday.
Pedro: So now we're even. *[He turns to Bruce.]* She's still gonna hit me again.

Laura, Hilda, and Nickie are standing together. Laura turns to Janice:
Laura: Hilda's mad at me.
Hilda: Yes, because you told me yesterday that you didn't love me!
Laura: I love you. I don't know why I said that.
They hug.

Students are lining up on a Monday morning. Hilda is first in line. This is 2017.
Me: *[to Hilda]* What'd you do this weekend?
Hilda: I spent all my money!
Me: *[figuring it out]* Oh, your birthday money. What did you buy?
Hilda: My Chemical Romance t-shirt, Guns 'n Roses t-shirt...

Monica: Mr. Henry, there was a catastrophe at my house this weekend!
Me: What happened?
Monica: The Wi-Fi went out!

Some students are playing foosball during lunch, and there's much screaming.
Monica: Shhhh. Mr. Henry will make us stop. We're irritating him.

Nickie: Everybody be quiet. No talking except the referee.

Hilda: If you want to talk, whisper.

Monica: *Callate!*

Hilda: No, a whisper is too loud.

Nickie: Quieter than a whisper.

Diego: What's quieter than a whisper?

Monica: *[shouting]* Just shut up!

All the students together: Monica!

Several of the girls are gathered around my desk during lunch.

Hilda: *[to Nickie]* I didn't finish my book last night, because first we went to the gym and then we got a box of pizza for dinner.

Nickie: Lucky! All I get to eat is qeenugh salad.

Me: You mean quinoa salad.

Nickie: That's it!

Hilda: *[to Nickie]* I never heard of it. What is it?

Nickie: It's like rice. It tastes like lemon, and it has cucumbers in it.

Hilda: Pizza sounds better.

Monica and Hilda are looking at their Chromebooks. Monica turns to me.

Monica: I'm watching *It!*

Me: How can you watch that on your Chromebook? It just came out.

Monica: I'm watching the first one.

Hilda: It's so much better. The new one is stupid.

Nickie: I know. The ending is so stupid.

Monica: You know what I hate about my little sister?

Me: What?

Monica: She takes a strawberry, squishes it in her hands, and rubs it all over my backpack. That's why I had to take everything out and clean it!

Hilda is showing me the novel she is writing on her phone and a group of girls, including Monica, are gathered around.

Monica: Mr. Henry! It's about me!

Me: Oh. *[I read the start of the novel.]* I like it. I like that the mother never cooks. But I think at some point you're going to have to get into that.

Monica: My mother never cooks!

Hilda: *[to Monica]* And you've never met your real dad. *[to me]* That's going to be in the book.

Diego: Mister, can we watch the Hammurabi rap again?

Me: *[to Diego]* We'll watch it at the end of class as long as you don't irritate me.

Monica: *[to me]* That'll never happen. Pedro is bound to irritate you at some point.

The class has been slow to come to order after a lively activity, and I have to chew out some students to get them to focus. Then I turn to Hilda and speak quietly to her.

Me: Man, I love that. You know what a drill sergeant is, Hilda?

Hilda: The guy in the army.

Me: Yep. Wouldn't that be fun?

Hilda: You'd be a good one, Mr. Henry.

Monica walks in and sees Hilda's new shoes.
Monica: No way! Great shoes!
Hilda: *[sad]* You wanna trade?
Monica: Why?
Hilda: My mom wouldn't let me get Converse.
Monica: Those are great!
Hilda: *[smiling]* You think so?

Monica: If you come to my house on the weekend, you'll see me in my pajamas.
Hilda: If you come to my house, you'll see me in a super big *Call of Duty* t-shirt and shorts and my hair hella crazy.

Previously Monica has told the class that she's sad because her dog, a pug, has died. She is standing with Hilda.
Monica: Mr. Henry, Hilda's mean! For a talking piece for the circle on Friday, she said I should bring my dead pug! *[I start laughing.]* Mr. Henry! It's not funny!
Me: I know. It's not.
Monica: But you laughed!
Me: Well, that's because...Well...
Monica: Well?
Me: Well...I guess it is sort of funny...I mean, that Hilda said it.
Monica: Mr. Henry!
Me: I'm sorry. It's not funny. And I really am sorry your dog died, believe me. It's crazy how much we love our dogs.

Monica: That's right! You said you still miss your dog! Would it be funny if you brought your dead dog to school?!

Me: No, it wouldn't.

Monica: *[to Hilda]* You see!

Hilda: *[sheepishly]* I still think it's kinda funny...

[The next day, this happens:]

Monica: *[to me]* This is what I brought for circle.

Me: What is it?

Monica: It's a dog toy.

Hilda: It's the one her dead pug used to play with!

Me: *[not sure how to react]* Oh, well...

Hilda: I still think the dead pug would be better.

Monica: Hilda!

Hilda has gone to see relatives in Texas over Winter Break. She sees Monica for the first time in my room.

Monica: How was Texas?

Hilda: It was so fucking racist! We were driving, and there was a traffic stop, and they let all these white-ass people go through, and then they stop us and say, are you American citizens? And I shouted from the back, 'Hell yes we're Americans!' And my dad told me he'd take care of it. *[after a pause]* Plus, it took days to drive there, and I almost got car sick.

Laura: My leg hurts, Mr. Henry.

Me: Why?

Laura: I don't know.

Me: When did it start?

Laura: I don't know.

Me: How bad is it?
Laura: Oh, I don't know...

Monica: Mr. Henry, did you hear about the huge pickle?
Me: No, I didn't.
Monica: He was a big dill.

Monica: Mr. Henry, what state has the smallest drink?
Me: I don't know.
Monica: Mini-soda.

Monica: Mr. Henry, watch this: *[into her iPhone]* Siri, tell me a pick-up line.
Siri: You auto complete me.

Monica: Mr. Henry, don't let Maria do one little task.
Me: Why not?
Monica: She hasn't been allowed ever since fourth grade!
Me: Why?
Monica: She made such a mess!
Me: That was two years ago. Do you think she's earned a second chance?
Monica: No!

The bell has rung to go to the next period, and everyone has left the room, but Hilda is still packing up her stuff. Monica is waiting for her patiently.

Hilda: I'm going to be late to class. Go ahead.

Monica: *[putting her arm around Hilda]* No, I'm not going without you. I don't care if I get a tardy.

Students are gathered in clusters in different places in the room during lunch. Suddenly, from one of the groups:

Diego: Man, that is fucked up!

Monica: *[who's in another group]* Hey, language!

Diego: Sorry.

Nickie: *[standing next to Monica]* Let's face it: Monica is everyone's mom.

The girls all nod.

Monica: Mister, can you please keep this? It might break in my backpack.

Me: What is it? *[looking]* Oh, a cake mix.

Monica: Hilda's going to come to my house after school, and we're going to make it!

Me: That'll be fun.

Monica: No, that'll be great!

Monica: Mr. Henry, I hate my mother more and more.

Me: Oh, Monica, why is that?

Monica: Oh, I don't know...well, she won't drive me, and she makes me walk. Like yesterday, she knew my legs hurt, but she made me walk to my grandma's.

Me: Couldn't you take the bus?

Monica: She won't let me take the bus! She's afraid I might get lices.

Me: You mean *lice*. She's afraid you might get *lice*.

Monica: Yeah.

Me: Wow. Parents are really irritating sometimes, aren't they?

Monica: Yes! Mr. Henry, they are!

Monica: Mr. Henry, my parents won't let me see *Ouija Board*. They say it will give me nightmares.

Me: Maybe they're right.

Monica: So what?! I already have nightmares. I can handle a few more.

Several students are playing foosball. Pedro has declared himself referee.

Pedro: Red card on Monica!

Monica: How can I get a red card!? I didn't injure a player! It's *foosball*!

Pedro: I'm the referee. I say you get a red card.

Monica: Okay. Referee, get out.

Another time:

Pedro: I'll be the referee.

Monica: No! You're a terrible referee. Bruce is the referee.

Pedro: I'll be the assistant referee.

Monica: As long as you don't do anything.

It's second homeroom, and Monica is watching Pedro write the day and date and which periods will meet for the next day on the white board, since not all periods meet every day.

Monica: Write bigger. *[He erases and writes.]* And fancier. *[He erases and writes.]* And neater. *[He erases and writes.]* Neater. *[He erases and writes.]* And that's not how you spell Wednesday.

Pedro: How do you spell it?

Monica: I'm not sure, but not like that.

Hilda is handling the collection of the Chromebooks, and I can't find mine.

Me: Is my Chromebook in the cart?

Hilda: Nope.

Me: It should be. What did you do with it?

Hilda: I didn't do anything with it. Remember, you took it out, because there wasn't a charger for it.

Me: That's crazy. I can't find it. It was in the cart. You're the cart monitor, so clearly you lost it.

Hilda: *[tolerantly]* Mr. Henry.

Me: I'm just teasing, Hilda.

Hilda: *[more tolerantly]* I know, Mr. Henry.

Me: I wonder where I put it...

Hilda: Probably the right drawer of your desk.

Me: Let's see...*[I open the drawer. It's there.]*

Hilda: You're welcome, Mr. Henry.

Laura: Would you rather have $200 or a party?

Hilda: Depends. Is it a great party?

The girls come back to visit at lunch on the first day of seventh grade.

Hilda: Mister! We have to take sex ed this year!

Monica: I already know everything! *[Laura sees a current student's work at what was her seat.]*

Laura: Mister! You let a boy sit in my seat!

Monica: The first day of sixth grade was the worst. I'm anti-social, and I ate lunch by myself.

Me: Didn't you go to elementary school with Hilda?

Monica: She deserted me!

Hilda: I couldn't find you!

Monica: So I sat next to some eighth graders. They didn't even talk to me.

The girls nod in sad silence.

They're in seventh grade visiting me in my room before school starts.

Nickie: Oh, no! I didn't get my math homework signed!

Monica: I'll sign it for you.

Hilda: I always sign my mom's name.

Monica: *[signing Nickie's paper]* Every kid cheats on the parent's signature. It's like a rite of passage.

Very upset, Hilda comes into the room.

Me: What's the matter, Hilda?

Hilda: I failed my notebook check, and that's why she gave me an F.

Me: What was wrong with your notebook?

Hilda: My Cornell Notes fell out. Just for that she failed me!

Me: It's the first report card. You have plenty of time to make it up.

Hilda: Mr. Henry! I get straight As! That's what I do!

Monica and Hilda were best friends throughout sixth grade, but during seventh grade they suddenly stopped talking to each other, even though they both come into my room during lunch. Then, for no apparent reason, the ice seems to thaw.

Hilda: Remember when we weren't talking to each other?

Monica: Well, you blocked me.

Hilda: I blocked everybody.

Monica: But that meant I was the same as everybody!

Hilda: But I didn't want to deal with anybody. Just...nobody.

Monica: You could have told me about it.

Hilda: *[after a pause]* I didn't know what I would say to anybody except nothing...

I know the seventh graders have gone on a field trip for science, and Monica and Hilda stop into my room.

Me: How was the field trip?

Monica: It was fun!

Me: The observatory, right?

Monica: Uh-huh. And people were taking our pictures!

Me: Tourists.

Monica: Mr. Henry, they were my fans!

Hilda: And I was invited to go on the field trip to UCLA this weekend!

Me: That's great. *[to Monica]* Are you going, Monica?

Monica: I've already been to UCLA. They'd see me and say, 'What are you doing here again?'

Laura comes into the room and walks around. She sees that the history vocabulary words are taped to the walls of the room as part of some activities we do to build vocabulary.

Laura: Mister, do you still need these words taped to the walls?

Me: Yeah, we're still learning them. Just like you guys did. Why?

Laura: I want to take them off and use the tape to stick them to Nickie's hair...

[She looks at them, realizes she shouldn't take them down, walks around the room, and leaves.

The next day, Nickie runs into the room during lunch, looks around, and gets on the floor behind some desks.]

Me: Nickie, what are —

Nickie: Ssshhhh! We're playing hide and seek! *[After a moment, Laura comes into the room.]*

Laura: *[looking around, acting way too casual]* Good afternoon, Mr. Henry.

Me: Hi, Laura. *[Laura looks around the room, spots Nickie, and goes over to her.]*

Laura: Got ya! I knew you'd come in here!

Nickie: *[in frustration]* Aaaahh!

The girls are standing in my room during lunch talking amongst themselves.

Hilda: My mom showed me a condom last night.

Monica: *[horrified]* She wants you to have sex?!

Hilda: No, she just wanted me to know about them.

Nickie: Why does she have them? I thought she wanted to have another kid.

Hilda: Yeah...

Nickie: *[to Hilda]* I thought you were thinking about being a lesbian.

Hilda: Yeah, I am.

Nickie: Then you wouldn't need a condom.
The girls all agree that's true.

Monica stops by at the start of eighth grade.
Me: Who do you have for English this year?
Monica: *[sadly]* Mr. Smith.
Me: What's the matter? He's a great teacher.
Monica: Yeah, but none of my friends are in the class.

Later she stops by again.
Me: What period do you have next?
Monica: History. Mr. Jones.
Me: American History.
Monica: Uh-huh.
Me: Where are you? The Constitution?
Monica: *[thinking]* No, we already had that.
Me: The Civil War?
Monica: I don't know. We watched part of a movie. It was definitely a war.

Soon the girls stop coming by, and I miss them and hearing about their lives. One of their last conversations was this:
Hilda: I have to take care of my little brother. It's so unfair.
Nickie: *[to Hilda]* Don't you have an older brother?
Hilda: Yes! And he never has to do anything!
Monica: I have older brothers.
Nickie: *[to Monica]* But their dad's not your dad.
Monica: No. My mom has four kids, but there's three dads. My

mom's a ho.

Me: Don't talk like that.

Nickie: And the first time she was raped, so that doesn't count.

Hilda: No, that wouldn't count.

The girls nod in agreement.

You're smarter? I got a 9/10, and you got 7/10. Nine is better than 7, dumb ass.

THE TYPICAL CLASS

YOU'RE RIGHT: THERE'S NO SUCH THING. JUST AS every student is unique, every class is unique. And no class is constant—eleven year olds are constantly changing, so a class made up of eleven year olds is constantly changing.

This class was typical in the sense that in the terminology of LAUSD it was an "English Only"(EO) class, which was the most common designation for students at that school at that time. EO meant, theoretically, that the principal home language for all students was some sort of English—African-American English, Chicano English, or more-or-less mainstream English. Typically, the Latino students in these classes were functionally bilingual, and unlike students in the English Learner classes they rarely spoke Spanish to each other.

It was also typical because it had a wide mixture of students. There were unidentified Gifted students, unidentified Special Education students, identified Special Education students, students who spoke Spanish at home but had officially become proficient in English, students with profound trauma in their pasts, and the unmotivated students who had little buy-in to the educational system and had few influences in their lives to change that—except for their teachers. This latter category of student had no concept of Growth Mindset or High Expectations or On The Path To College, and it was their teachers' jobs to undo a lifetime of being disappointed by adults and acquiring learned helplessness and transform that into a belief in a brighter future.

Teachers confronted this impossible task in varying ways, and, sadly, eventually empathy for students' difficult lives waned due to what is called "compassion fatigue."

Clyde is a likeable-enough boy who displays little interest in anything academic. His parents never come to any school functions, and he never talks about life at home. He is rarely a huge behavior problem, and he tests at about a third-grade reading level, which puts him a little below average for that class. It has become became incredibly frustrating trying to find ways to motivate him, so I try this approach.
Me: Come on, Clyde. Let's get started. You know what, Clyde? Focus, try your best, and surprise me so much that I have a heart attack. *[to the class]* Wouldn't that be great? That I'm so astonished by Clyde really trying hard that I have a heart attack and die?
Much of the Class: No! That would be terrible! *[various comments]*

Me: No, it would be great. Really. You'd be my age, old and grey, and you'd still remember the day when your sixth-grade teacher dropped dead because Clyde tried to do his best.

Somehow this strikes a chord. The students turn to each other and talk about whether they'd remember it or not and whether it would be cool or horrible.

When students misbehave, some teachers think that calling home is the most effective measure. One of the key things a teacher has to learn is for which students it works and for which it's pointless. Some parents are unreachable, some parents are as lost as you are in terms of to what to do for/about/with a child with chronic and serious behavior issues, and some parents can turn things around quickly. I disliked calling home because usually it didn't result in any serious change and because I found it undercut my ability to demonstrate that I was in charge of the classroom, which is the same reason I almost never referred a student to the Dean. Here are students' reactions to me mentioning that an action or statement might be worthy of a call home, which was typically an idle threat.

- "Aw crap—that's another e-mail home."
- "Mister, don't call my mom. I'll be good, I swear."
- "Go ahead, call my mama. When you find her, let me know."

It's second homeroom, and the students have five minutes of free time on their Chromebooks before they have to turn them in. Many of the boys are playing Fortnite.

Juan: Stand up if you're a beast at Fortnite. *[Many of the boys stand up.]* Reggie, sit down.

Johnny: Yeah, Reggie sit down. *[Reggie sits down.]*

Susan and Nelly are in the classroom at lunch, and Susan is watching Nelly draw on the whiteboard.

Susan: I'm going to the bathroom.

Nelly: Okay.

[Susan starts to go, and Nelly keeps drawing.]

Susan: You're not coming?

Nelly: No. Just go fast.

Susan: Come on.

Nelly: I don't want to.

Susan: Okay.

[Susan walks out the door, and the door closes, and Nelly keeps drawing.

Then Susan walks back in.]

Susan: You really weren't coming!

Nelly: No, I don't want to.

[Susan sulks as she walks around the room and Nelly continues to draw.]

Susan: Okay. I'm going. But I'm not coming back.

[Nelly doesn't say anything, just keeps drawing. Susan walks out. The door closes. A moment later Susan comes back in.]

Susan: I can't believe you!

[Nelly keeps drawing on the white board.]

Susan: Nelly, let's go!

[Nelly shows off her drawing.]

Nelly: Isn't this pretty?

Susan: No!

Nelly draws, and Susan sulks for a while. Eventually Nelly heads out, and Susan follows her.

S1: Mister! I saw a rat last night in my bedroom! *[Immediately several students start talking about rats.]*

S2: That's nothing. My cousin woke up, and there was a rat on the table next to his bed!

S3: My dad got out his pistol once and shot a rat!

- What's the matter, Monica? You look sad.
- Oh, you always have your reasons why you shouldn't be happy in the morning.

Emily and Juan are doing partner work, reading a piece of text together, making an assertion, and then finding evidence to support the assertion.

Emily: You ever been to court? I don't know what to wear.

Juan: Never been.

Emily: You ever met a lawyer?

Juan: Nope. And I never will.

Emily: You never know.

Juan: I'll never commit a crime.

Emily: Mr. Henry, you think Juan will ever commit a crime?

Juan: *[before I can answer]* Actually, I will commit a crime. I'll shoot you in the head. Now can we please make an assertion about this text?

Brad is talking out of turn.
Me: Louis, knock it off. *[Brad keeps talking.]* Louis, I said stop. *[Brad keeps talking.]* Louis! Stop!
Louis: What did I do?
Me: Oh, sorry, I meant Brad. Brad, shut your mouth.
Louis: Why'd you yell at me?
Me: I meant Brad. I confused nouns. Get over it. Old people do it all the time.
Devin: No, Mister! You not old, you 'hood!

I call on a boy. He gets the question right.
MS: Look at me! I'm a banger!

The class is lining up, having had P.E. the previous period.
Me: How was P.E.?
Diego: A bunch of butterflies flew by. It was cool. But some kids thought they were wasps.
Me: So they started screaming?
Diego: Yep. Mostly girls. Mr. Henry, why do girls scream a lot?

MS: Mister, I can't stand Georgina! She plays too much.
Me: Like what?
MS: Like soccer! She pinches you during a soccer game! You don't pinch in soccer!

Students are doing a writing project on their Chromebooks, and I'm going around the room giving the students the same direction—that the pronoun "I" has to be capitalized. Finally, I can't stand it.

Me: Okay, everybody stop. Eyes on me. *[I wait. Finally, the students stop working and look at me.]* You are not texting. You are writing something for school. You must capitalize the word "I." Every time. You cannot write like you're texting. You're driving me crazy. Capitalize the word I. Every time. Got that? *[The class says they understand.]* Seriously. You are making me lose my mind. Is that what you want? You want to be known as the class that drove Mr. Henry crazy?

The Class: *[various comments]* Yes! Wouldn't that be great! We'd be legends! etc.

Diego: *[running into the room during lunch]* Mr. Henry! They're not going to fight after all.

Me: *[taking a guess]* That's too bad. Nothing beats a good girl fight.

Diego: I know! They just go crazy!

We're doing a map exercise covering Asia. A boy asks me how his map is so far.

Me: Well, you've colored China blue. Remember, only water is blue. So you've flooded the whole country of China.

MS: Mister, you didn't hear about the tsunami?! It covered all of China. So my map is right!

Class is ending. One girl, Stephanie, has been sleeping most of the class. My policy usually was to let them sleep; a common belief in education is that students can fulfill their secondary needs such as education only after their primary needs of food, shelter, and rest are met.

Me: Stephanie, sleep at home, not in class, okay?

Stephanie: *[angry]* I couldn't sleep at home! I had to go to the hospital!

Me: Why'd you go to the hospital?

Stephanie: My dad broke his hand!

Me: How'd he do that?

Stephanie: Skateboarding. I broke that thing in two for him.

Me: Why'd you have to go with him?

Stephanie: Because no one was home to take care of us. They have a kids section at the hospital. There's computers and stuff.

Me: You couldn't stay home and take care of your sister? You're about old enough.

Stephanie: No, there's this crazy lady next door. It's a long story.

A group of girls are sitting around at lunch. One girl takes out a bag of Hershey Kisses and hands them to her friends.

FS: Man, I love chocolate. I wish everything was chocolate. I wish my house was chocolate.

FS2: I wish I was chocolate! Then when I got hungry, I could just break off a piece of me and eat it!

Then there is much discussion about how cool that would be, but it would have to grow back, etc.

Me: Emily, don't hit Joaquin every time you walk by him.

Susan: You know, Emily, that means you like him.

Emily blushes.

As the bell's about to ring:

Juan: I have to go pee again.

Me: Juan, don't share that with us.

Juan: Oh, sorry.

Mr. Henry, over the summer I helped make a scarecrow on my uncle's farm in Mexico.
It turned out really scary!
Even though I helped make it, it made me afraid!

FS: Mister, I'm sorry I threw that book at that boy, but he was annoying me.

Me: Apology accepted. But you didn't have to throw the book, you *chose* to throw the book.

FS: No, I had to.

Me: No, you chose to.

FS: No. He's that annoying. I *had* to.

MS: Mr. Henry, isn't it horrible to be an adult and have to work all the time?

MS: Mr. Henry, when you grow up, do you still have time to play?

Minimum days are very short days, ending at 12:30, which typically precede holidays or follow parent conference nights and happen about ten times a year.
Emily: Mister, when's the next Minimum Day?
Me: End of the month. Why?
Emily: Well, on Friday, Juan and Susan and I went to 7-11 and bought a pizza and Slurpees and had this great food fight! We said we'd do it again the next Minimum Day!

Class is over, and the students are leaving. Don't forget, they're eleven.
Me: Hey, Stephanie, nice gold nails.
Stephanie: They're not gold.
Me: They sure are.
Stephanie: No. *[pointing to another girl's nails]* Those are gold nails. *[holding up her own nails, to me, with derision]* These are rose gold.

Juan: Mr. Henry, have you ever seen *The Bye-Bye Man?*
Me: Nope.
Juan: Well, don't! It's so stupid!
Me: Okay, I won't.
Juan: It's about this guy...*[and Juan details the whole plot.]*
I'm taking the class to the library to check out their books for reading time. Juan picks up a stick.
Me: Juan, drop that stick.
Juan: Okay, but I'm going to break it in pieces first. I love breaking

stuff.

Me: Everybody does. You ought to go into demolition as a job.

Juan: No! I'm going to go into doing absolutely nothing as a job!

On Thursdays one year we had Staff Theme Dress Day, where someone would pick a theme, and those of us who wanted to would dress in that theme. It could be Sports Gear Day, Stripes Day, whatever. Toward the end of school, it was Dress Like You're On Vacation Day, and I wore lime green shorts, a bright Hawaiian shirt, and a pink fedora. I'm talking in History class about the importance of the Roman Republic and how it formed the basis for our government. Suddenly a girl bursts out laughing.

Me: Brenda, come on.

Brenda: *[trying not to laugh]* I'm sorry, Mr. Henry, but I just can't take you seriously dressed like that! *[And she laughs some more.]*

Brenda: Some days I can be good, Mr. Henry. But other days, I don't know, I just can't do it.

Me: Yeah, I've realized that.

I am out several weeks on medical leave. When I return:

MS: Mister, thank God you're back!

Brenda: I know. I play around a lot, but it was so much worse when you were gone!

Me: Brenda, Melissa is absent, and I need someone responsible to take care of the Chromebooks, so do it for me, okay?

Brenda: Well, if you need someone responsible, don't ask me!

The period is about to end, and we're lining up to leave. Max, who has been misbehaving during the period, apologizes.

Max: Mister, I'm sorry I was talking like that.

Me: Apology accepted. Max, I love that you work hard and get everything done, but when you do, then read your book. Don't start talking to other people. You're keeping them from doing their best.

Max: I know. Besides, Francisco's a poo-poo head, and I don't really want to talk to him.

It's been raining. First Charlie comes in, soaked.

Charlie: Mister! I took a nature shower!

Then Doug comes in, also soaked.

Doug: Mister! I was playing in the Cochran Pond!

Emily: Mr. Henry, can I change seats?

Me: Why?

Emily: Cause in the other class Richard sits in my seat.

Emily: Mr. Henry, I have to wash the dishes every night!

Me: Oh, *pobrecita...*

Emily: I know, right?!

We have a uniform policy: students have to wear a white or a grey polo shirt and dark blue pants, shorts, or skirts.

Me: Victoria, where's your white, collared shirt?

Victoria: I have one.

Me: Go get it.

Victoria: It's in my backpack.

Me: Then put it on. *[She puts it on over her t-shirt. This happens nearly every day.]* What's so bad about white, collared shirts, anyway?

Victoria: They're itchy, they're stupid, and they're ugly.

Me: You know, I bet if I said you could wear anything else, but you could *not* wear a white-collared shirt, you'd probably want to wear one.

Victoria: *[after thinking]* Probably. So?

Emily and Victoria come to the door, wearing their uniform shirts, a rare occurrence.

Me: Hey, you two are wearing your uniform shirts even after P.E.!

Emily: *[smiling]* Yeah. We're trying to do better, Mister.

Me: Great idea!

Victoria: *[not sure]* Yeah, I guess so...

Victoria walks by, out of uniform, going to another class.

Me: Victoria, where's your white-collared shirt?

Victoria: In my backpack! Where else would it be?

Victoria: Mister, is Friday a vacation?

Me: Yep, no school. Cesar Chavez's birthday.

Victoria: Aaugh!

Me: What's the matter?

Victoria: I hate vacations!

Me: Why?

Victoria: Because there's nothing to do! That's why I come to school. Because it's something to do.

Me: Does your mom let you ride the bus? You could go to the beach.

Victoria: Ride the bus?! She barely lets me cross the street!

Juan: When does spring break start?

Me: This Friday.

Juan: Really? So what does that mean?

Me: It means there's no school next week.

Juan: What? No school the whole week?

Me: Yeah. It happens every year. Spring break.

Juan: Really? I don't remember...

The class is working in groups on a history assignment as I sit on a stool in the front of the room and watch. To no one in particular:

Me: So how was the sub yesterday?

Esperanza: He sent Tracy out for no reason!

Me: He sent out an angel like Tracy for no reason?

[The class laughs. Tracy, who is quite possibly my favorite student, is anything but an angel, and she smiles. I turn to Tracy:] So what did you do?

Tracy: Well, we started to do the assignment you left for us, and I said I didn't understand it, and somebody, I won't say who *[as she turns to look at Pepe, the class shouts out "Pepe!"]* said I couldn't read. So I said I sure as hell can read, and threw my book at him, and the sub told me to get the book, and I did, and then he called the office anyway. Then they called my mom, but when I told her the whole story. She wasn't that mad.

Francine is absent, and I ask her best friend Emily if she knows where Francine is.

Me: Emily, did you hear from Francine today?

Emily: *[sadly]* No.

Me: *[surprised]* No? Why not?

Emily: We had a fight, so she blocked me on Snapchat. So I blocked her texts.

[The next day, the two girls are sitting together.]

Me: *[to Francine]* So why did you block Emily on Snapchat?

Francine: We had a fight.

Me: About what?

Francine: I can't remember.

Emily: *[to Francine]* I was hanging out with Kate.

Francine: Yeah, that's right.

Emily: But now I'm not.

Me: So everything's cool.

Both girls: *[smiling]* Uh-huh!

I'm standing outside the door as the children are arriving for the day. Bob sees Donny.

Bob: Hi, Donny.

Donny: I'm not here. I'm in virtual reality.

Bob: Okay. *[He kicks Donny.]*

Donny: OW!! What are you doing?!

Bob: You're not here. You're in virtual reality.

Tracy walks up to me during homeroom.

Tracy: Mr. Henry, do you have a rubber band?

Me: Really? Is that how you get what you want in life?

Tracy: Sorry. *[starting again]* Mr. Henry... Fuck! I forgot what you say!

Me: May I –

Tracy: Got it! Mr. Henry, may I please have a rubber band?

Me: Yes, you may. *[I give her a rubber band.]*

Tracy: Thank you.

Me: You're welcome. And next time clean up your language.

Tracy: Sorry.

Pete walks in during lunch

Pete: Hi, Mr. Henry.

Me: Hi, Pete. What's up?

Pete: I was betting people a dollar I could crack my nose.

Me: Okay…

Pete: I won a dollar. Some people wouldn't pay up.

Me: Well, don't bet with them again.

Pete: I let them give me chips instead. *[He sits down and plays with his Chromebook, then gets up. On the way out:]* I'm going to go win some more money.

I take roll and notice that Preston is absent. I ask if anyone has heard from him.

MS: He won't be here today. He's going to stay home and play games all day. A new one came out.

The first bell has rung, and the students are gathering outside the room. They have ten minutes to get into the room and into their seats. Sam walks up, speaking to the crowd at large.

Sam: Did you see that video?

Josie and most of the others: Yeah!

Josie alone: Where the mom comes into the room and says to the kid, 'What the fuck are you doing?!'
Sam: And the girl says, 'Nothing'!
Josie: And the mom says, 'Well stop fucking doing it, bitch!'
And the whole group breaks into laughter.

I'm humming, for whatever reason, "Falling in Love Again," as I walk around the class, checking in on them as they work on a group project, discussing it amongst themselves. Then I sing faintly, "Falling in love again, never wanted to…"
David: Mister, what's that song with 'falling in love' in it?
Me: There's gotta be tons of songs with that lyric.
David: The one by the guy who died at 42.
Me: *[thinking]* Forty-two…Well, there's one by the Spinners, but I think they're all alive.
David: Something about fools, too.
Me: Oh, Elvis. *[I sing the song.]*
David: It's called "Falling in Love With You."
Me: No, it's not.
David: Yes it is! I'll bet you a dollar.
Me: I don't bet with students. Look it up. But if you're wrong, you wash my car.
David: What do you think it's called?
Me: "Fools Rush In." *[We both look it up.]* It's called, "I Can't Help Falling In Love With You."
David: Ha! I'm closer!
Me: Yes, you are.
David: Whew! I don't have to wash a car!

Roberta, who has been feuding with her former bestie Esther, walks in with "Happy Birthday" balloons and gives them to me.

Roberta: Hi, Mr. Henry. These are for Esther. You give them to her. I don't want to.

I'm playing Chet Baker's Live In Paris *album during homeroom.*

David: *[to Sam]* My Grandpa listens to this kind of music.

Sam: Mine too. *[And then Roberta walks in.]*

Roberta: Mr. Henry! What kind of music is this?!

Me: Jazz.

Roberta: Mr. Henry! I got you!

I've been playing a Bud Powell song during a test, then I turn it off.

MS: *[sadly]* Ohhhh, I liked that song. *[later, the same student, as Byrd's "Mass For Four Voices" is playing during a test:]* Wow. What's the name of this song?

MS: Mr. Henry, what time is it?

Me: Look at the clock.

MS: It takes too long for me to figure it out.

Me: You mean you can't tell time on a clock that isn't digital.

MS: I can too! I just don't want to.

Me: See, if I tell you the time, it's what's called enabling: I'm helping you remain a lousy time-teller. I'm actually helping you if I *don't* help you.

MS: Mr. Henry, that makes no sense at all. *[And he walks out of the room without looking at the clock.]*

Mother's Day is approaching. I ask the class if they want time during history class to draw cards. Liz pipes up.

Liz: No thanks, Mr. Henry. I stopped giving my mom cards when I realized she just threw them out afterward.

Others in the class nod. No one wants to make cards, and we go on with reading The Bronze Bow *by Elizabeth Spear.*

The girls who are friendly with Marcie have decided that they don't like her anymore, and, now ostracized, Marcie is continually sad and alone. During class one day, she asks to go to the bathroom, and I let her go, and as she walks out she passes by the girls. Gracie turns to her.

Gracie: Hey, Marcie.

Marcie: *[Marcie stops and looks at them and smiles. It's on her face—'Yes! I'm back in the group!']* Yeah?!

Gracie: We still don't like you.

[Marcie's smile disappears, and she heads out.]

In sixth grade in LAUSD typically a teacher teaches two groups the same, or close to the same, content. Eventually the two groups get to know each other, and this is what happens. Invariably it's only girls who do this.

Gracie and Fredi come into the room; Gracie is in one group, and Fredi is in the other.

Gracie: This is my seat. Who sits here?

Fredi: Pedro.

Gracie: Oh no!

Fredi: This is mine. Who sits here?

Gracie: Bobby. *[The two girls smile; this is apparently a good thing.]*

Fredi: How about this one?

Gracie: Carlos.

Fredi: Too bad for Janey!

And the two girls go on comparing notes…

MS: *[in the middle of English class, apropos of nothing]* Mr. Henry, is fog clouds?

Me: What's wrong with the way you wrote "sixteen"?

FS: Nothing!

Me: Really?

FS: *[fiercely]* Yeah, nothing!

Me: Really?

FS: *[looking at what she wrote]* Oh. The "t" in the middle shouldn't be capitalized.

Me: Right. *[I look at the student.]*

Student and Me: *[She sighs, and we say together]*: The Third Commandment: read it over before you turn it in.

FS: *[proudly]* Hey, Mister: I have a *strategy* for questions six, seven, and eight!

We're discussing Hammurabi's Code.

Me: So, overall, what would life be like without any laws?

MS1: It would be like *The Purge!*

Me: Exactly. And you know what, pal? You're gonna be first on my list.

Rest of the Class: Oooooooooohhh…

MS2: No, me! Make me first on your list!

MS1: No, me! He said me!

MS3: No, me!

And the boys keep arguing about which of them I should hunt down and kill first...

I try making the class do online typing lessons until I realize that the tables at which they sit are too high for students to type well. During the typing lessons:

- Aaaahhhh! I want to throw this across the room!
- This is so frustrating!
- This is actually good. It gets you frustrated and makes your brain go, "Aaahhhhh."
- Why is this so hard?
- Why does this get harder?

Pedro, if you were a girl, would you go out with yourself?

Ummm...

Okay, if you were a girl, and Rodrigo asked you out, would you go out with him?

Ummm...   Boys are useless.

THE GIRL CLASS

I TAUGHT ONE CLASS THAT CONSISTED OF TWENTY girls and five boys. At that time my school was using a block schedule, which meant there were three two-hour blocks of instruction every day. Clearly whichever "Educator" thought this up never taught in an urban middle school (if anywhere): for everyone involved, spending two hours straight in a room with twenty-five–thirty-five adolescents is a bad idea. And if most of those adolescents have significantly imperfect home environments, it is a nightmare waiting to happen—or, actually, happening daily. (A friend taught at an exclusive and expensive private middle school; they had 45-minute classes.) To compound the situation for this class, we met after lunch, which is always problematic with sixth graders. Despite all this, I have extremely fond memories of this exasperating group of children.

It helped that my room was next to the cafeteria, which I regularly used for any number of activities. It was also a pure block, meaning it was exactly the same group for both classes, so I had flexibility about which subject (history or English) to teach that day.

It was an English Only class, about half black and half Latino. Over 90% qualified for free or reduced lunch, and, according to LAUSD data, about eighty percent came from homes with either one or zero biological parents present. (Cochran Middle School was in an area LAUSD calls "the kin care corridor"—a strip of Los Angeles with a profoundly high ratio of formal and informal foster care arrangements.)

The predominance of girls made me realize I had a pro-girl bias; I loved their energy and passion. EVERYTHING mattered. Sometimes it was Hammurabi's Code, sometimes it was Hot Cheetos. A bad hair day meant that a girl was going to have a tough time learning anything. If something had happened at lunch, then unless we confronted it, we'd have a pointless and stressful two hours. Fortunately the girls liked each other, and, as I remember it, we had no serious fights or altercations in the class—although I also remember being fed up some days because there just was no interest in, say, the ancient civilization of the Indus River Valley. But generally we got along, had some fun, and more or less covered the assigned curriculum. At the very least, we made it out alive. I ended up feeling sorry for the boys, who were outnumbered and were, overall, not as high performing as the girls. The girls knew this and had little patience when the boys exhibited their academic shortcomings.

MS: My teeth fell out!
Felita: What? You lost all your teeth?
MS: No. Just one!
Felita: Then why'd you say *teeth*, dumbass?

MS: What month is this?
Maria: April.
MS: April? I thought it was July.
Felita: July we're on vacation!
MS: Really? Wow...
Felita: *[muttering]* You fucking moron...

Rhoda and a boy are doing partner work, a map-reading exercise where they have to read the map and answer questions.
MS: *[to Rhoda]* I can't find the answers!
Rhoda: *[looking over at his history book]* You're using the wrong map, dumb ass!

Elaine and a boy are doing peer editing, where they check each other's papers for mistakes.
MS: You spelled that wrong. You're stupid.
Elaine: *I'm* stupid?! You're stupid! You don't even know what 12 x 11 is, so shut the fuck up! Shit, I'm 20 times smarter than you! *[going on the attack]* What's 12 x 9? *[no reply]* What's 12 x 13? *[no*

reply] What's 12 x 15? *[no reply]* See! I'm 80 times smarter than you!

During History, as the class works in pairs, reviewing a series of questions before a test:
MS: *[to Claire]* Who the fuck is Lao-tzu?
Claire: The founder of Daoism, dumb ass!

Me: Okay, take out your books, everyone.
MS: Are we going to read?
The class erupts: "Nooooo." "Oh, come on." "You really asked that?"

Felita: Ew, you farted!
Tanya: Ew!
Marcia: Ew!
Me: Knock it off, everybody.
Diego: *[not the farter]* What's the big deal about farting, anyway? Everybody does it.
Silence. They all think about that.

The class comes in after lunch. During the first activity, which teachers call the dispatch, or bell work, or something similar— something simple for students to do to get them focused—it's clear there's something going on. I go to the front of the room.
Me: All right. What's going on?
[There's buzzing and whispering among the girls. Finally, one girl stands up.]

FS: Mr. Henry, Candi got kissed at lunch! *[The room explodes into talking as Candi smiles and blushes.]*

Me: Candi, was this against your will?

FS: Oh hell no!

Me: Candi?

Candi: No. He was saying thank you. I gave him some chips, and he kissed me on the cheek.

She blushes, and the room explodes again. I stand back as the girls go back and forth about what happened. For a good five minutes—which is an eternity in a classroom—I just stand and watch. Eventually everyone settles down, and we get on with schoolwork.

Felita: Mister, I have to do all this?

Me: Yep.

Felita: *[complaining]* Oh, Mr. Henry...

Me: Oh, *pobrecita*...

Felita: Mister, stop calling me *pobrecita*!

Me: Don't act like a *pobrecita*, and I won't call you one.

Felita: Mister!

Beth is looking in a mirror and putting lipstick on.

Me: Beth, put the mirror away, please.

Beth: Hold up, Mr. Henry; I got to make myself look pretty.

FS1: Mr. Henry, I need your opinion, and be honest: does my hair look weird?

Me: It looks fine.

FS2: It's pretty!

A girl has changed her hair into an elaborate updo.

FS1: *[admiring the hair]* Wow! Who did your hair?

FS2: I did. It was hard! To put long hair on top of your head and get it to stay there...

FS1: You should open a salon!

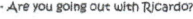

- Are you going out with Ricardo?   - I don't know. Ask him.   - I did. He said he doesn't know.

We're doing an activity where the pretense is that the Zombie Apocalypse has hit, and groups of students have to prioritize a list of items they're left with and which of the various people in a fictional group of professions are most important. One group of girls has elected to keep people like a female beautician and a teen-aged girl instead of a male doctor and a male police officer.

Me: Why did you leave those people behind?

FS: Because they're boys!

During a boys-only, girls-only activity:

FS: Mister, get these boys out of here. They're ruining our vibe.

Me: Marcia, it's not too late in the year to fail this class.

Marcia: What grade do I have now?

Me: A "D".

Marcia: That's a good grade!

Me: No, it's not. In fact, you should be ashamed of and embarrassed by your lack of effort.

Marcia: *[with a tone that says, 'You poor, misguided soul']* Oh, Mr. Henry...

I take away Felita's bottle of spray perfume that's sitting out.

Felita: Mister, no!

Me: I'll give it back to you after class. Trust me, I don't want your perfume.

Felita: Then why'd you take it?!

Me: Because some knucklehead boy will take it and spray it around the room.

Felita: Oh. Yeah, you're right.

Esmerelda: Or they'll spray it in somebody's eyes.

Felita: Yeah, they would.

Me: Don't forget I have it. Because I will.

Felita: I won't.

FS: *[very excited]* Mr. Henry, my mom gave me some perfume!

Me: Why?

FS: Because my aunt gave it to her, but she didn't like it. She only likes the one my dad likes.

The subject of a parent's age at a child's birth comes up in the novel we're reading.

FS: Mister, if my older sister is 21, and my mom is 35, how old was my mom when my sister was born?

Me: Do the math. What operation would you use?

FS: Ummmm...subtraction.

Me: So subtract.

[She does the math, and she's shocked.]

FS: But... I'm 12...*[She is stunned, seeing what it means. Then the rest of class does the calculation, too.]*

FS2: Yo mama a ho! *[Some students laugh.]*

Me: Knock it off!

There's a moment of silence, and then quickly everyone starts talking and doing their own calculations. I sit down and watch them, and they eagerly share the information they've learned; I ignore the planned lesson, and the calm, curious sharing goes on for ten minutes.

I can't find the materials for a planned activity. After searching the room, I finally find them.

Me: Sorry about that delay. I know you're all heartbroken to lose that two minutes of instructional time.

FS1: Heartbroken?

Me: Your hearts are broken because you missed two minutes of my fantastic instruction.

FS1: My heart ain't broke 'cuz of that.

Me: So, let's go. *[I see that a girl is still talking to a classmate.]* Quiet, please, we're moving on.

FS2: Sorry, Mr. Henry. I was heartbroken, so I had to talk it out.

- Mr. Henry, my friend is so fucking annoying!
- Language, please.

But she is!

During a unit on Buddhism, students have to keep a journal and see if they follow the steps on the Eightfold Path, such as Right Speech and Right Conduct. Then they have to write an essay and describe where and how they are good Buddhists or bad Buddhists.

S1: This is good. It makes me look at my life.

S2: If I want to be a good Buddhist, I have to stop cussing.

I'm at my desk correcting the essays while the students are working, and I read Maria's essay, which has the line, "I did not use Right Conduct when I put my baby brother in the oven."

Me: Maria, come here, please. *[She comes to me.]* You don't need to make stuff up. Putting your baby brother in the oven?

Maria: I did.

Me: What?

Maria: Yeah. My Grandpa was bugging me, so I got my baby brother and put him in the oven 'cause I knew it would get Grandpa mad.

Me: *[believing her]* And then?

Maria: Then he couldn't find him. It was great!

Me: And then...

Maria: Then I told him. He was so mad!

Me: *[almost afraid to ask]* You didn't turn the oven on, right?

Maria: Mr. Henry! I'm not crazy!

FS: Right Conduct, I get. But why is cussing not Right Speech?

FS: I had the Right Attitude part, anyway. I mean, I didn't really *mean* to do bad stuff and cuss all the time...

FS1: *[showing a girl a broken fingernail]* It broke.

FS2: How?

FS1: I was playing volleyball.

FS2: No! You never play volleyball with fake nails!

I get a new student who's very, very short. He's also newly arrived from Central America, speaks no English, and is very quiet and shy. The girls are now in seventh grade, and they come into my room one day before school to say hi, and they see him.

FS1: 'Sup, Mr. Henry! *[seeing the boy]* Is that a sixth grader?! Ooohh! He's so cute! [The other girls squeal, along with "I don't believe it!" "He's so cute!" "Really, he's a sixth grader?"] Let's go look at him!*

Me: Girls, go to homeroom.

FS2: Let us take him home, Mr. Henry!

Me: He's not a souvenir. Go to class.

FS3: You're no fun, Mr. Henry!

FS2: Bye, Mr. Henry!

The girls leave.

The class is very talkative and has a hard time focusing. I'm upset, and the bell rings to end the period, and they start to gather their things.

Me: Stop. No one leaves until someone explains this to me.

All the students groan and complain—typically this is an "exit ticket," a question about something we discussed or something students must do before leaving the classroom. I stand and wait, and soon there's silence.

Me: So. I want to know why, even though you guys really irritate me, I still like you.

The class bursts into happy talking and shouting.

FS1: Because we love you, Mr. Henry!

FS2: Because we're awesome!

ALICE AND BETTY

ALICE AND BETTY WERE BEST FRIENDS WHO DID everything together—played on the same soccer team, ate lunch together, walked home together. Alice was always upbeat and energetic and uncensored, which meant she was often a pain in the neck, something she admitted to me when she reached eighth grade. Betty was quiet and reserved. Of course, I loved them both, as they were delightful children, the kind I got to teach, not the kind I got paid to teach.

Betty and Alice walk in together on Monday morning. Before they say hello:

Alice: *[disgusted]* Mister! We tied on Saturday!

Betty: And their goal wasn't even a goal! It didn't cross the line, but the ref said it crossed the line!

Alice: And then I used my shoulder on a girl! *[proudly]* I'm a savage! *The girls slap high fives.*

Betty: Then later, the girl fell down all by herself, and he called a foul on Alice!

Alice: He wore glasses, so I said he needed new glasses! So he got mad.

Betty: *[to Alice]* We were better than they were!

Alice: *[to Betty]* We were! *[Another high five.]*

Me: Good morning, girls.

Alice: Good morning, Mr. Henry.

Another morning they're chatting as they walk into class.

Alice: Hi, Mr. Henry. *[to Betty]* I hate Mr. Smith so much.

Betty: Me too.

Another morning I learn there was a fight the previous day after school involving one of my students, but I know few of the details.

Alice: Mister! You hear about the fight yesterday?! My homey stood up for me!

Me: A girl fight? *[I look at shy and demure Betty, who smiles and nods.]* I love a good girl fight. They really mean it. *[Betty, still smiling, nods again. I look back at Alice.]* Who was in it?

Alice: *[pointing at classmate Trish, who's walking in]* Trish!

Me: *[turning to Trish]* Did you win?

Trish: Hell, yeah. All she did was pull my hair.

Me: *[to Trish, trying to judge the intensity of the fight]* Did you take off your earrings?

Trish: No.

Alice: [to Trish] Girl! You gotta take your hoops off!

Alice and Betty come back to the class after lunch.

Alice: Mr. Henry, during soccer, I got kicked in the leg!

Me: That's too bad.

Betty: I kicked a girl in the shin. I didn't mean to, but she deserved it anyway, cuz she was bossing me around. Just because she's thirteen doesn't mean she gets to boss the game.

Alice walks into the room with Betty.

Alice: [to me] Why is the world so cruel!?!

Me: What's the matter?

Betty: Alice forgot her sweater.

Alice: Mr. Henry, where's your favorite place in the world?

Me: The Cote d'Azur, in southern France.

Alice: I have a new profession. I want to be a photographer. I'm going to go around the world and take pictures of cool places.

Me: That's great.

Alice: You know, like a cool picture of the Eiffel Tower. Have you ever seen one?

Me: I've seen the actual tower. Go on your Chromebook and search for restaurant Jules Verne. J-u-l-e-s V-e-r-n-e. It's in the tower. [She does so; she and Betty look at the photos of the food and the view from the restaurant, which is part-way up the Eiffel Tower.]

Alice: Wow!

Betty: [sadly] I could never afford to go there.

Me: I can't either. My friends went and told me about it.

Alice: I'm going to take pictures just like those! Oh, and Mr. Henry, I'm not going to be an angel anymore.

Me: What?

Alice: I'm going to be a killer clown.

Me: What? *[I thought we were still on professions, then I realize that Halloween is approaching.]* Oh, for Halloween.

Alice: Yeah. I have the blood make up, and I'm going to do my face. It's going to be great!

Me: What's your weapon?

Alice: A sword. No, I mean a knife. A bloody knife. It's going to be great! And it's next Tuesday!

We're doing a superhero comic book project, and Alice, Betty, and I are discussing superheroes.

Me: Wait, so Wonder Woman can be killed?

Alice: Sure. She's killed all the time.

Me: How can anyone be killed more than once?

Betty: Because she lives in the multi-verse.

Me: What?

Alice: The multi-verse.

Me: What's the multi-verse?

Alice: Where people live. Like the universe.

Betty: Lots of universes.

Me: I'm really confused.

Alice: It's the multi-verse, Mr. Henry!

Now in seventh grade, Alice is walking with Betty across the yard.

Alice: *[to Betty]* That bitch gave me an "F" for no reason. *[Alice sees* *me and waves frantically, smiling broadly.]* Hi, Mr. Henry!

Me: Hi, Alice!

Alice: *[to Betty]* For no reason! I fucking hate her!

You're annoying. You know that, right Diego?

JESSICA

JESSICA WAS ANOTHER OF THOSE HIGH-ENERGY, heart-on-her-sleeve, uncensored girls whom many teachers disliked specifically for those reasons. I found her endearing, mainly because she was honest about everything. Like many of our students, she had an unhappy home life and few adults who would listen to her.

Students are lining up Monday morning. I turn to Jessica.
Me: How was your weekend?
Jessica: Pretty good, I guess.
Me: What'd you do?

Jessica: Saturday was Monique's party, and Sunday I slept all day.
Me: Her birthday?
Jessica: No. Confrontation or something.
Me: Confirmation.
Jessica: Yeah, that's it. And Communion. At St. Paul's.

Jessica: Don't ruin my weekend, Mr. Henry.
Me: Jessica, when I put in a call home and say you didn't do your homework, I'm just telling the truth.
Jessica: Don't! The truth is death!

Jessica: Mister, what time do we leave?
Me: When I say so. Here's a crazy idea: just do the assignment and time will go faster.
Jessica: Mister! I don't like doing work!

Jessica: *[arriving in the morning]* It's a great day, Mr. Henry! My mom broke up with her boyfriend!
Me: That's good, huh?
Jessica: That was my dream!
Me: So I guess dreams do come true.
Jessica: Yes, they do!

The bell to end the day is about to ring, and students are straightening up. I turn to Jessica.
Me: So what are you going to do today, when school's over?
Jessica: Get the clothes and go to the place and do the laundry.

Me: Laundromat. It's called a laundromat.
Jessica: Yeah, that place. That's my Wednesday.

Francesca: Jessica, are you still seeing Pablo?
Jessica: No! I'm single! And I like it!

Jessica: Bye, Mr. Henry. Have a great weekend.
Me: You, too, Jessica. Read a good book.
Jessica: No! How could you say that?!

The students are silently doing an online reading activity on their Chromebooks. Suddenly Jessica blurts out her thoughts.
Jessica: Mr. Henry, why is my screen so dirty?
Me: I don't know. I guess you're a slob.
Jessica: I'm not a slob! You got the wrong person! The real slob is in the front row!
The whole class: Roberto!

FS: Mr. Henry, this whole Chromebook/Schoology thing sucks.
Me: Why is that?
FS: My mom uses Schoology to check my grades every day!
Jessica: My mom doesn't care about my grades. She just cares about the rent.

Jessica: Mister, you didn't shave.
Me: Nope.

Jessica: You overslept.

Me: Yep.

Jessica: You should shave every day, Mister.

Me: You're probably right.

Jessica: Yeah, I'm right.

It's now seventh grade, and Jessica often returns to stop by and chat before school. The first bell has rung, and students have ten minutes to get to their rooms before school starts. Jessica walks up to me, and she doesn't look happy. I offer my fist, and we bump fists.

Me: What's up?

Jessica: Nothin'.

Me: You seem sad.

Jessica: Stuff at home.

Me: Oh, that's bad. You can't do anything about it, can you?

Jessica: Nope.

Me: That's when it sucks. When it's out of your control. *[There's a moment of silence; I'm just nodding in agreement.]* I'm sorry. *[Another silence as Jessica nods; after a moment:]*

Jessica: Thanks, Mr. Henry.

We bump fists again, and she goes to class.

Jessica is walking by the room, and Michael runs by her and taps her on the shoulder.

Jessica: Fuck you, Michael!

Me: Watch your mouth.

Jessica: Mister, I can't watch my mouth. I got to be sayin' those words!

Another seventh grade morning before school.

Jessica: Mister, can I come to you for homeroom?

Me: Sure. *[I start writing a note.]* Go to your teacher and say, 'Excuse me, Mr. Smith, but may I please go to Mr. Henry's for homeroom? Here's a note from him saying it's okay.'

Jessica: Mister! I can't do that! I can't talk like that! You know me!

Me: Yeah, but isn't it time you learned?

Jessica: Mister! Never!

Another morning.

Jessica: Hi, Mister.

Me: Hi Jessica. What's up today?

Jessica: Nothin'.

Me: Where's Blanca? *[her best friend at the time]*

Jessica: She's gonna meet me at homeroom.

Me: Read a book last night?

Jessica: Mister, really?

Me: You ought to try it sometime.

Jessica: Yeah...Bye, Mister. See you later. *[She starts to leave.]*

Me: Bye, Jessica. Hey, Jessica. *[She turns around.]* Look up this expression during homeroom: 'The world's your oyster.' Look it up.

Jessica: 'The world's your oyster.'

Me: Yep.

Jessica: Sounds weird.

Me: Come back and tell me what it means. 'Cause it can be true for you.

Jessica: *[clearly intrigued]* Okay...

The next day. She stops by again before school.

Jessica: Hi, Mister. I looked up that oyster thing. I can get what I want.

Me: Yep. You're smart; you've got spirit, great personality...Learn to read better, and learn some math, and the world's your oyster. *She looks at me, nods, and we bump fists.*

-You were gone a long time!
-I had to tie my shoes!

MICHAEL AND PATRICK

MICHAEL WAS A HIGH-PERFORMING SIXTH-GRADE autistic student who preferred to eat lunch in my room, away from all the noise and commotion. Patrick was a Gifted student I had for homeroom for all three grades. (At one time teachers stayed with the same homeroom for sixth through eighth grades.) In many ways the two boys could not have been more different—different grades, very different home situations, different racial backgrounds—but they ate lunch together for a number of months. It started as a matter of circumstance, because they were both in my room at the same time, and sometimes they were the only students there, but they became friendly and shared their lives and their observations. Eventually they even started playing the Pokemon card game together.

Patrick was living with his aunt when I met him in sixth grade, and his mother was out of his life, but after she emerged from rehab she visited him sometimes, which, naturally, affected him in complex ways. When he was in seventh grade, she died, and partly because Patrick knew that my parents had died, he would often talk to me about losing a parent and ask questions about it. He often ate a Hot Pockets or something similar for lunch, which he warmed up in my microwave. Michael was very bright and had the character traits of most autistic children.

Michael: [while eating lunch, out of nowhere] Mr. Henry, was Hitler a Christian?
Patrick: I saw it on the History Channel. He was.
Michael: He sure didn't act like it.

Michael: There's one thing I don't like about the Romans, Mr. Henry.
Me: What's that?
Michael: If there's a weakling, they leave them to die. That's not nice.
Patrick: Like that book you gave me to read, *The Boy of The Painted Cave.*
Michael: [who is reading that novel in my History class] Exactly. What happened to Tao. Cavemen I expect it, but the Romans ought to be better than that.
Patrick nods.

Michael: [walking in to eat lunch] Mr. Henry! Our unit in P.E. is tennis!

Me: That's cool.

MS: I know! Now I've played it for reals and the Wii!

It's St. Patrick's Day, and I'm wearing a green shirt.

Michael: Are you Irish, Mr. Henry?

Me: I have some Irish ancestors.

Michael: Do you drink a lot?

In eighth grade Patrick and a few friends come into my room to play foosball during lunch. There is the usual shouting and trash talking, which reminds me of my college experiences with foosball. Some things never change. But sometimes academic conversations take place. Patrick and his friends have stored their Science Fair projects in my room, and they're examining each other's work.

Sam: That's weak, bro. Dr. C. gonna say your data don't have nothin' to do with your hypothesis.

Patrick: He's right.

Sam: And bro, "loses" is l-o-s-e-s; you spelled loose. Like it ain't tight. Which has nothin' to do with your experiment.

Michael: Oh my God, Mr. Henry, I hate P.E.!

Me: Why?

Michael: Either you run or you do nothing, and Michelle hits everyone.

Michael: I like you, Mr. Henry, but I don't like Mr. Smith.

Me: Actually, it's not important to me that you like me. I want you

to learn from me. And Mr. Smith cares a lot whether you learn.
Michael: Okay, I don't like you. I love you.

Michael: Mr. Henry, are you glad you work at a school?
Me: Sure.
Michael: I mean, really happy? Really happy when you stop and think about it? You're glad you work here?
Me: [*reflectively, after thinking about it*] Yeah, I am.
Michael: Good. I'm glad, too.

Michael: You know, Mr. Henry, sometimes when I'm reading, I forget I'm in this classroom.
Patrick: That happened to me last week in English. It's great.
The two boys nod.

By eighth grade Michael stops coming around as much, but one day he comes rushing in at lunch time to see me, the day before a California gubernatorial election, looking extremely upset.
Michael: Mr. Henry, who should I vote for tomorrow!?!
Me: What do you mean?
Michael: Tomorrow is the election, right? And I don't know who to vote for!!
Me: That's okay. You can't vote. You're too young.
Michael: What?!
Me: In America, you have to be eighteen to vote.
Michael: [*immensely relieved*] That's good. I have no idea who to vote for!

Patrick comes in to warm up his Hot Pockets. I take it from him and put it in the microwave. He waits a moment before he speaks.

Patrick: Did you ever see your father after he died, Mr. Henry?

Me: You know, I did. I was walking down the street where I grew up, visiting my mother, and I had the impression that my father was in the sky, looking down on me.

Patrick: I saw my mother last night, Mr. Henry.

Me: Where were you?

Patrick: In my room. I was sitting on my bed, and I looked up, and she was standing in front of me.

Me: Did she say anything?

Patrick: No. *[The timer bell on the microwave rings, and I take out his Hot Pockets and give it to him.]* Thank you.

Me: You're welcome.

Patrick: She was smiling.

Me: Good. How did you feel?

Patrick: I wasn't afraid or anything. It was okay.

Me: Good. You know, I'm sure she loved you very much. I know your aunt loves you very much.

Patrick: Yeah.

He sits down and eats his Hot Pockets.

Diego, come back here. You don't even run in P.E.!

THAT ODD MOMENT...

TOMAS, A BOY FROM THE SIXTH-GRADE AUTISTIC class for students whose behavior keeps them out of the general education setting, stops by my room. I don't know his name, but I've seen him around, and I know why he's come to see me: he has warned me that a group of boys have been bullying his friend Mikey, who is also autistic and who is one of my students.

Tomas: Hi, Mr. Henry.

Me: Hi. You know, I don't know your name.

Tomas: Tomas.

Me: Hi, Tomas. Don't worry: I'm watching those boys.

Tomas: Good. You know what the big issue is in the world, Mr.

Henry? Communism.

Me: Oh.

Tomas: Look what happened in 1962 because of Communism.

Me: What, exactly?

Tomas: And you can't blame the Cubans, either. They wouldn't have done anything if it weren't for the missiles in Turkey.

Me: *[catching on]* Well, that was only part of it.

Tomas: Bobby Kennedy was a hawk. That was the problem.

Me: *[still trying to get over my amazement]* Well...Do you know how far it is from Turkey to Moscow?

Tomas: *[with certainty]* One thousand miles.

Me: *[I have no idea, but that sounds close enough.]* And how far is it from Cuba to the United States?

Tomas: *[again with certainty]* Eight hundred miles.

Me: No, it's more like eighty. So Russia having missiles in Cuba is not the same as us having missiles in Turkey.

Tomas: I'll have to think about that. Bye, Mr. Henry.

He walks out, and I realize this is the first time I've ever heard a student mention Communism, Turkey, 1962, Russia, the Cuban Missile Crisis, or Bobby Kennedy.

I always have used a method for partner work where the students made three appointments—one o'clock, two o'clock, and three o'clock—and then sat back down, and I randomly picked one of the numbers. In this instance, a boy did not get the cute girl in the class as his partner.

MS: No! I didn't get Elizabeth!

Another boy, after making all his appointments:

MS: Look! I got all the smart kids!

I'm walking across campus, and I see a former student.
Jocelyn: Hi, Mr. Henry.
Me: Hi, Jocelyn. How many people have you hit today?
Jocelyn: *[thinking]* Just Pablo. He pulled my hair.

- Screw you, Pancho!
- Evelyn, do me a favor: Make yourself look good and sound smart.
- Not that again

MS: Mister, are we ever gonna go on a field trip?
Susana: Why would we? Look at us!
Me: Well, since you brought it up... Susana's right. I mean, look at the way you behave. Do you guys really think I'd even want to take you around the block? I mean, think about it. *[Silence in the room.]* I can't even trust you to walk to the library without causing trouble. You think I'm going to take you out in public?
More silence. Most of the class nods.

Students line up to come in. Larry, who never comes to class with so much as a pencil, holds out his hand for me to shake it.

Larry: Sup, Mr. H Dogg my nigga. *[We shake hands.]*

Me: Larry, let me show you a real handshake, from Berkeley, in the '70s.

I demonstrate the three-step handshake that was the hip routine at my high school.

Larry: [nodding] Cool.

He goes into class. From that day on, that's our handshake.

During eighth grade homeroom, Christina storms in halfway through the class.

Christina: That motherfucker says I need anger management! *[I start laughing. Christina turns to me.]* What's so funny?!

Me: Well, maybe he has a point.

Christina: Oh yeah?!

Me: *[smiling, looking at her]* Well, your language, for example.

Christina: Oh, sorry, Mr. Henry. But he pisses me off!

Me: I believe you.

Christina: Aaaahhhh!

Another day Christina comes in late to homeroom.

Christina: Sorry I'm late, Mr. Henry. *[She gives me an official excused note.]* I was in the Dean's office.

Me: What'd you do?

Christina: Nothing.

Me: Really? Nothing?

Christina: Yeah, nothing. I was talking to Mr. Smith out on the yard.

Me: *[guessing]* You mean you were *yelling* at Mr. Smith.

Christina: Well, yeah. In class he was all up at me because I didn't do my homework. Like that's going to get me to do it or something.
Me: Ah. So you approached him on the yard to respectfully broach the topic of whether it was productive of him to address you in class with a reprimanding tone.
Christina: Exactly! And then Ms...what's her name? Oh, yeah, Ms. Jones, she comes over and tells me not to talk to an adult like that. And then she says, 'And who are you, anyway?' So I said, 'I'm Christina Delgado. Who the fuck are you?' And she says, 'I'm Ms. Jones. Anything else you want to say to me?' And I said, 'Yeah: You're fat and you got big tits.' So she sent me to the Dean. I mean, she started it! All I did was answer her question!

Two girls pass by my room as I'm standing at my door.
FS1: That fuckin' Jonathan.
Me: Watch your mouth.
FS1: Sorry, Mr. Henry.
FS2: *[to FS1]* Yeah, watch your fuckin' mouth.

FS: Mister, I was thinking of ditching next period, but I decided it's a bad day to end my no-ditch streak.

FS: Oh, Mister, I just know I'm going to get into a fight today.

You know, Mr. Henry, people say they're tomboys,
but they're not: they're afraid of insects.

SOCCER

FOR OVER TEN YEARS I SUPERVISED THE AFTER-
school soccer program at my second middle school. It was officially
an anti-gang program, and although there was not a strong gang
presence at the school for most of that time, the program kept the
students occupied on the soccer field instead of getting in fights at
the nearby Jack-in-the Box, which sporadically was a trouble spot.

The students called me coach, but that is an insult to real
coaches. I often had young assistants who were employees of the
after-school program. They were typically former high school
soccer players, and the first thing I tried to get them to understand
was that soccer wasn't the point. Our mission was to attract and
keep precisely the kind of players who would never make a soccer

team—not because they weren't good enough, but because their grades and inability to listen to an authority figure would prevent them from lasting past the first practice. As a result, we rarely did drills or ran laps and instead just scrimmaged. Sadly, few players went on to play in high school, despite my constant urging to get them to go to class in high school, get good grades, and play high school soccer. My greatest success was a boy, who also happened to be my sixth-grade student, who, after coaching with me as part of a high school internship program, went on to get a four-year, full-ride soccer scholarship to a small college, from which he graduated. I didn't improve his soccer, but I often told him he could have a great future if he worked at it.

To appreciate some of this you need to know that:
- we rarely had a lined field
- in the middle of a real soccer field there's a large circle where the kickoff takes place, and the defense must stand outside it
- when I forgot to bring a coin, we chose the first possession of the game by having the captains for the day choose a number between one and ten
- FIFA is the international organization that sets laws and standards for soccer
- Neymar is a Brazilian player who many perceive to be a crybaby

COMPASSION

Everyone is standing around looking at Julio, who has fallen awkwardly and is writhing on the ground in pain. The assistant coach and I kneel next to Julio and ask how he is. He starts crying. Diego walks up.

Diego: *[to Julio]* Come on, Neymar, get up. You ain't hurt. *[Julio cries louder.]* Man, yesterday, at home, I fell and broke my nuts, and I didn't even cry.

Bruce: *[looking at Julio, but to Diego]* That ain't even possible. You can't break your nuts.

Me: I think that is correct. I believe it is impossible to fracture a testicle.

Assistant Coach: *[trying not to laugh]* Yeah, Coach, I think you're right.

Diego: *[indicating Julio, who's still crying]* Well, it really hurt, and I didn't do all that crap.

And he walks away in disgust as Julio continues to cry.

One Player to Another: Love you, man. No homo.

Player One: I heard you broke up with Felita. Now you're all alone.
Player Two: Just like you.
Player One: No, I got your mama. And don't worry, I'm giving her *plenty of attention.*

Player One: Pass it to Black Bear. *[a black boy]*
Player Two: *[the black boy]* No man, I'm Yogi Bear.
Player Three: *[to Player Two, with the wisdom of the ages]* Yogi Bear's brown, bro.

ATHLETIC SKILL

Player One: *Aqui!*

Player Two: Don't pass it to the gay boy.
Player One: Yo mama the gay boy!
Player Three: That don't even make no sense.

Player One, a black boy: *[to a sweaty player after a bad shot]*
That's crap, you sweaty bear.
Player Two: Least I ain't no black bear.
Player One: Yo mama a black bear.
Player Three: That don't even make no sense!

MS: Pass me the ball. *[The ball does not come to him.]* I repeat, pass
me the ball!

AFTER BAD SHOTS

- "Man, that on the gay wall of honor."
- "I tried to do that, that's why."
- "I just ate, that's why."
- "I can't play well in this blue uniform. It distracts me."
- "I'm too fast, that's why."
- "The sun was wrong, that's why."
- "I was thinking about yo mama, that's why."
- "Brown Bear bothered me, that's why."
- "This ball is whack!"

MS: *[after a good shot]* Look at that! I'm all titties!

SOCCER ADVICE

Player One: Not like that – *mas duro*.

Player Two: *Tu mama es mas duro*.

Player Three: That don't make no sense, bro.

MS: [*to a male goalkeeper, after allowing a goal*] Next time, use your titties.

MS: [*to a captain who's about to pick a number between one and ten*] Bro, if you go first, it's all about picking five.

MS: [*when a player shoots too far away from the goal*] No, Diego, don't reach for the stars!

JOKE-TELLING

Player One: Diego, you like *pane* bread?

Diego: Huh?

Player Two: No, he likes *queso* cheese.

Player One: *Leche* milk.

Player Two: *Papas* fries.

Players One and Two dissolve into much laughter.

It's a rainy afternoon, so the soccer boys come to my room for a foosball tournament. The boys divide into two-person teams, and I make them name their teams.

Diego: I named our team Mac 'n Cheese.

Me: I like that name.

Diego: It's after my favorite food, that's why.

Bruce: [*his teammate*] How about lasagna?

Diego: Lasagnas.

Bruce: The Lasagnas!

COMPLIMENTS

Player One: Look at Diego run. He's actually using his legs. I'm very proud of him.

Player Two: Mr. Henry, did you see that big giraffe run? He ran like a human!

ENCOURAGEMENT

MS: [*to a teammate, before a penalty shot*] You don't make this, you're not a Mexican.

MS1: [*to another player, as the player prepares to take a penalty kick*] You have to know you're going to make it. Know it. *Know* you're going to make it. KNOW it.

MS2: I know you can suck my dick.

A player on the opposing team has taken a long shot. Bruce turns to his teammate Diego.

Bruce: Diego, use the Force on it! [*Diego points at the ball, but it goes in the goal.*] Your Force isn't strong enough, Diego.

LINGUISTICS

[one Latino to another] Nigga, I asked you to manage my Slurpy, not drink it.

ECONOMICS

MS: Bro, gimme a dollar.

MS2: Do I look like I have any money? If I did, I wouldn't be here.

MALE MODESTY

MS: I can't take my shirt off. Everyone will see my big titties!

CONFIDENCE BEFORE A PENALTY KICK

MS: Mr. Henry, get ready for magic.

GOOD COACHING

While Felita plays goal, she talks on the phone, and a very weak shot goes by her.

Me: Felita, come on.

Felita: Can't you see I'm on the phone!

We're about to start the daily scrimmage with the kickoff at the middle of the field, and I once again tell the players on defense that they have to get outside the imaginary circle in the middle of the field, but no one backs up.

Diego: They're not getting this 'big, round circle' concept, Coach Henry.

Sometimes we had faint lines left from a game played on weekends at the school. Just to make sure, I'd call a close ball out or say, "Play it!" There's a play way down the field, and I yell, "Play it." Diego is standing next to me.

Diego: That was out!

Me: You can't see that. It's fifty yards away. And we don't even have a line at that end.

Diego: I have FIFA technology. I know people!

DEALING WITH FANS

Mariana comes by soccer practice. She walks in front of the goal and starts talking with/criticizing/flirting with the goalkeeper Bruce, who tries to look around her and see where the ball is. She keeps talking to him and moving so she's blocking his view of the field. He doesn't complain and instead just keeps moving so he can see. Diego walks up to her.

Diego: *[to Mariana, overly solicitous]* Good afternoon, Mariana. Could you please stop interfering in our scrimmage and distracting our goalkeeper?

Mariana: Screw you, Diego.

Diego: And I would like it if you would refrain from such language.

Mariana: Fuck you!

Diego: *[shaking his head]* Sad. Sad.

He walks away.

Felita looks at him, starts to say something, doesn't, and then sits down quietly behind the end line, next to Bruce and the goal.

- Okay, who's staying after school for tutoring today?

- I can't. I have soccer practice.   - I can't. I have Folklorico practice.

- I can't. I have Fortnite practice.

THE COCHRAN CUP

We're about to have the annual game I started, the Cochran Cup, where students (the Cougars) and alumni (when needed to get a win) play against current and former teachers and staff.

Usually it is a big deal. There is a trophy at stake. One time we have the JROTC Cadets parade and say the Pledge of Allegiance, and the Fife and Drum Corps play. When we have a cheerleading team, they perform. Friends and family usually turn out, and a few times teachers who have left the school come back to play. While it never has turned into the homecoming style event I envisioned, it always means a lot to the students, who get to play against, and usually beat, their teachers.

This particular time the assistant coach, a young man who goes by "Coach J" and is an employee of the Youth Services division of LAUSD, and who will be the best player on the field by a factor of fifty if he plays, has decided to play for the teachers/staff team against the students he coaches, instead of coaching the student team while I referee.

I am upset at the young man, and I try to point out that a) he's deserting his team, b) they need his tactical instructions during the game, and c) now I have to ref and coach, so it's going to be tricky to make sure all the students get to play. But he's adamant, and after talking to him I walk back to the student team, disgusted. The team has gathered to start the game, and Jose sees that Coach J is putting on a faculty uniform.

Jose: Is Coach J playing for the teachers?

I nod, and muttering under my breath, I say, "That dickhead." Jose immediately turns to the rest of the team.

Jose: Coach J is playing for the teachers and Coach Henry called him a dickhead!

Now he has everybody's attention; the whole team walks over and stares at me.

Me: No, I didn't. *[I realize this goes against one of my rules, 'No Secrets & No Lies.']* Well, yes, I did, but you weren't supposed to hear it. It's a bad word, and you shouldn't say it. But if he's going to play against his own team, then I guess he is one.

Jose: He's a dickhead!

The whole team: Yeah, he is! He's a dickhead! *[There's much angry shouting, including gleefully yelling the word 'dickhead.']*

Me: Okay, enough. He is one. But don't use that word. He's a... 'dh.' Say, 'dh.'

Jose: Yeah. Don't say, 'dickhead.' Say, 'dh.'

Boy 2: *[to Jose]* Don't say dickhead, you dh!

Jose: You're the dh!

Boy 2: No, you are! You said, 'dickhead.' Coach just said we shouldn't say, 'dickhead,' we should say, 'dh,' and you went ahead and said, 'dickhead!' You can't say, 'dickhead,' you have to say, 'dh!' *[The whole team is saying to each other, "Don't say, 'dickhead,' say, 'dh, you dh'—and 'dickhead' is suddenly the best word in the English language.]*

Me: Okay, all right, everybody knock it off. Let's just go out there and kick some butt. Come on, huddle up. *[The team gathers in a circle, and we all put our hands in the middle.]* Remember: play hard and have fun. 'Cougars' on three. *[I pause—then, oh why not?]* Then dickhead. One, two, three. *[And the team lets loose with the biggest "Cougars!" and "dickhead!" ever heard.*

I walk to the center of the field and blow the whistle to get everyone lined up. My colleague, a teacher at the school and a close friend who often plays with the students to stay in shape and who is the staff captain, walks up me, confused.]

Colleague: Henry, did you guys just yell 'dickhead'?

Me: Yeah. Long story. Tell Coach J he can pass but he can't shoot. *I blow my whistle, and the game begins.*

Take out your homework, Panchito.

Mr. Henry. I'm on this planet to enjoy life, not to do homework

EPILOGUE

Wise teachers enjoy and celebrate the sorts of conversations you've just read, and generally that's where it ends, since middle school students rarely come back to visit. Every now and then I'd hear about former students, or they'd contact me. I mentioned the one former student who came back to assist me on the soccer field as a senior in high school. Another former student went on to a local community college and then came back to observe me teaching as part of a project he had to complete to get his AA degree; and when he visited to set up his observation schedule, he surprised me with the great news that he had gotten a full ride scholarship to a prestigious eastern university.

Or, of course, we'd hear about the other end of the spectrum: the boy other teachers and I had warned everyone about being incorrigibly dangerous who got arrested for attempted murder; the boy whose brother told me he had dropped out of high school after a year because he had three kids to support; the boy who was shot and killed while robbing a liquor store after sixth grade. And I lived near the second school where I taught, so I'd see former students in the neighborhood—and I even taught alongside a former student who went on to become a teacher.

My first commandment was Read, Stop, Think, Respond, which I came up with when someone asked me what the secret to being a good student was. I thought about the idea and came up with that slogan. I became so convinced that this was the key to success in school and in life that for a couple years I had students write it underneath their headings on their papers. I quit doing that when I saw that they were writing "R, S, T, R."

And then I got an e-mail from a former student who was in high school: "Hi Mr. Henry. Thank you for 'Read, Stop, Think, Respond.' I still think about it every day."

Who knows, maybe that is all it takes.